10p

PUF

Edi

WIN

THE MOONC

Joan Aiken's stories are all touched with magic, packed with action, bristling with strange events and curious and splendidly dramatic characters, whose vitality almost lifts them off the page into real life. So it is not surprising that she has now written two plays about mysterious, lonely places and the odd characters and pressures that build up in them.

Winterthing (which was first performed by the Puffin Club, see cast on page 8) is a poetic, haunting tale interspersed with foreboding, wintry songs that set the scene as surely as the summer songs of lovers in *As You Like It:* clearly, say these songs, there is going to be no easy escape for the four children, Jakin, Rendall, Lem and Carilan when they bring their exasperating old aunt to a deserted island off the coast of Scotland to keep her out of prison. Even there she finds something to steal, this time a baby – or is she, in some unknowing corner of her mind, saving them all from the deadly 'Winterthing', the time when the island is so swallowed up in winter that it disappears from mortal sight?

Sabretooth Lighthouse is the setting for the other play, *The Mooncusser's Daughter*, where irascible old Saul refuses to let any human soul come near, even his own daughter. But beneath the lighthouse lies a secret treasure, and certain villains are planning to steal it, come what may . . .

For this edition the plays have been edited and supplied with acting notes by the producers who first staged them. These plays are also great fun just to read, and after that there are all Joan Aiken's Puffin novels, to enjoy as well: *The Wolves of Willoughby Chase*, *Black Hearts in Battersea*, *Night Birds on Nantucket*, *The Whispering Mountain* and *The Cuckoo Tree*. For readers of eleven and over.

JOAN AIKEN

Winterthing and The Mooncusser's Daughter

TWO PLAYS FOR CHILDREN
WITH MUSIC BY
JOHN SEBASTIAN BROWN

PUFFIN BOOKS

Penguin Books Ltd, Harmondsworth, Middlesex, England
Penguin Books Australia Ltd, Ringwood, Victoria, Australia
Penguin Books (N.Z.) Ltd, 182-190 Wairau Road, Auckland 10, New Zealand
First published by Jonathan Cape 1973
Published in Puffin Books 1975
This edition copyright © Joan Aiken, 1973
Winterthing text copyright © Joan Aiken, 1972
Music copyright © John Sebastian Brown, 1972
The Mooncusser's Daughter text copyright © Joan Aiken, 1973
Music copyright © John Sebastian Brown, 1973

Caution

WINTERTHING *and* THE MOONCUSSER'S DAUGHTER are the sole property of the author and are fully protected by copyright. They may not be acted by professionals or amateurs without formal permission and the payment of a royalty. All rights including professional, amateur, stock, radio and television broadcasting, motion picture, recitation, lecturing, public reading and the rights of translation in foreign languages are reserved. All inquiries should be addressed to the author's agent:
A. M. Heath & Co. Ltd, 35 Dover Street, London W.1.

Made and printed in Great Britain by
Hazell Watson & Viney Ltd, Aylesbury, Bucks
Set in Monotype Garamond

This book is sold subject to the condition
that it shall not, by way of trade or otherwise,
be lent, re-sold, hired out, or otherwise circulated
without the publisher's prior consent in any form of
binding or cover other than that in which it is
published and without a similar condition
including this condition being imposed
on the subsequent purchaser

For Kaye Webb with love

WINTERTHING

This play was first presented at the Young Vic, London, on 17 January 1970. It was produced by John Phillips for the Puffin Players. The cast was as follows:

Jakin	*Aaron Lewin-Poole*
Lem	*Matthew Line*
Rendall	*Jenny Cromwell*
Carilan	*Clare Dannatt*
Auntie	*Nicola Kingsley*
Goat	*Belinda*
Mrs MacRoy	*Sally Mates*
Sedna	*Ariadne Stark*
A Stranger	*Richard Rogers*
Also appearing	*Louisa Young*
	Adam Stout

NOTES BY THE PRODUCER

ABOUT THE PLAY

Winterthing is not a fairy tale. It has its roots in northern mythology; Sedna is, in fact, an Eskimo goddess, and Joan Aiken has only slightly changed her attributes. In the far north, where it remains dark for five months of the year, they used to believe in the Gods of Winter and Summer, and that it was possible to placate them and communicate with them; the Northern Lights, with which the play ends, were thought to be one of the ways in which the Gods showed themselves. We may laugh at such ideas; but have *you* ever been by the sea when a gale is blowing, or been caught in a thunder-storm, or marvelled at a spectacular sunset? You don't have to be an Eskimo to be impressed by such things; everyone feels them, and that's why *Winterthing* works.

The key to the play is this feeling that there are happenings which can't be explained simply in scientific terms. Joan Aiken brings together very ordinary things, like catching fish, with the very unordinary story of the island; the unexplained finding of a baby mixed up with boiling some potatoes. So the play must be treated in a very matter-of-fact manner, or the magical bits won't seem extraordinary; every time Jakin scoffs at the idea of the Winterthing, it brings the audience back into touch with reality, and makes the next bit of weird business much stronger.

THE CHARACTERS

One of the problems with *Winterthing* is that it seems so real, and the story is so believable. This makes great demands on the actors, who, though they are mostly playing children's parts, must not be childish, but totally convincing. So it is important to match the actors as far as possible to the characters in the play, and fortunately Joan Aiken has given us very clearly defined ones.

Jakin is the practical one, who can turn his hand to anything, but ends up a different boy from the one we see at the start of the play.

He has to change from an energetic doer to a boy who has given up.

Lem the dreamer has a strain of practicality underneath, and this becomes clearer as the play progresses. He is more impressed than the others – even Rendall – by Mrs MacRoy's tale, and seems to be slightly psychic. He has to sing, but don't worry too much about that; the songs (which are lovely by the way) can be shortened or even done by someone else if it's absolutely necessary.

Carilan is a little horror, and we always know exactly where we are with her. It's probably the easiest of the children's parts, as it's always simpler to act nasty than nice.

Sedna doesn't talk, but that doesn't mean she doesn't act. She needs to stand still and not fidget – not easy to do. But her importance is much larger than her silence suggests. If she always watches closely the action on the stage she will give the impression of being slightly eerie without being sinister.

Auntie could be played by a grown-up, if there's a spare one about. She can be made into quite a funny character (you can even add a few lines to suit the person playing her) but don't let her become a complete figure of fun, or you will have spoiled the reality of the play.

Stranger bluff and nautical. Again could be a grown-up.

Mrs MacRoy a hard part for a child; try not to make her too witch-like at the beginning, or you'll give the game away. And when she turns into Winter, she *must* speak her lines in quite a different way; if she's a goddess she should jolly well speak like one.

THE SETTING OF THE PLAY

The stage

How you decide to set this play will depend to a large extent on the type of stage you have. If it is a traditional stage with a *proscenium* (that is an arch across the front behind which the curtains run) you may want to treat the play exactly as in the script, and divide it up into different scenes by pulling the curtains each time, perhaps while Lem is singing one of his songs, and the stagehands move the scenery safely out of sight. But if your stage is quite a large one, it is probably better (and much quicker) to have both the inside and outside of the cottage on the stage all the time, and separate the parts of the action by bringing the lights up and down; the cottage interior could be on the right-hand side of the stage, and the outside on the left. (Theatre people when talking about left and right, usually mean the left and right from the actors' viewpoint – exactly the opposite to the audience.) As there are only seven people in the play, and they aren't on all at once, even quite a small stage can be used this way.

If you have an *apron* stage, or a *theatre-in-the-round*, you can do the same sort of thing, and perhaps expand the outside/inside idea to include having the sea in front. One of the problems with these 'open' kinds of stages is that you don't have any curtains, so you must use your ingenuity to make scenery that requires very little alteration for the various scenes (two acts).

The setting

One exciting thing about the play is that it doesn't need elaborate scenery. When the children first arrive with their aunt, the house is dilapidated; this means that the audience can actually watch the actors 'build' the cottage. Not literally, but just hanging up curtains, making tables and benches (we had a pile of old beer crates on the stage which were made into tables, beds and so on). A stage which has appeared bare and unpromising can be transformed in front of the audience to a croft on a barren island.

The *cottage* itself should be kept fairly simple. The chairs, table, and a few bits of curtain can make a very convincing interior. If you are lucky enough to be able to have Carilan's room up on a balcony (it doesn't need to be very big) you will find it a great help; it's always useful to have split levels on a stage, as people then don't mask (get in front of) each other. And you can have fun with her being chased up and down by Jakin. Auntie's alcove can be just as described, with a thin piece of curtain on a few rings which she can pull behind her when she goes in. As for the walls and door of the cottage, we didn't have solid ones, but suggested them by hanging ropes. You can do something like that, or just have some light frames for doors and windows. It may sound funny, but the audience very quickly get used to the idea that there isn't really a door, just a place that is always used by the actors to go out and in.

What you do need in the cottage is a central point, and we used the fire. It was a small pile of sticks with a red light beneath and was placed on the floor downstage (that means near the audience – upstage is the opposite, towards the back of the stage). The advantage of this is that when everyone is gathered by the fire they can still be facing the audience without looking unnatural. And of course, the red light shines on their faces and looks very real.

Outside should be kept as simple as possible. We had one rock about eighteen inches high and made of polystyrene; the rest of the scenery was left to the imagination of the audience, helped of course by the actors. We had a sort of apron stage, with a step down of about three feet at one point, so we made the high part into the island, the low part the sea. So when Jakin goes fishing he dangles his line over the edge of the raised part, and everyone knows there is water below. There was a large area between the raised part and the audience so, when the sea was frozen, we stretched an old gauze cloth across, and it looked just like ice. If your stage has a similar space, you can try all sorts of experiments, with Jakin walking off across the ice, the 'Pretty Rogue' coming over the sea; even the whole family arriving with Mrs MacRoy at the beginning, sailing boat and all.

If your stage has a cyclorama cloth (a tightly stretched cloth which runs round the bank of the stage and which can be lit to look like the sky) this will help to give the feeling of space needed for the outside scenes.

Lighting

This is important in a play like *Winterthing*. In fact, in the Puffin Players production it was *the* most important thing for giving the atmosphere. We had the cottage area always lit by a warm orangey glow, while the outside was a bit bluey and chilly, getting chillier as the play went on. If the action was taking place indoors then the blue light was faded down; if outdoors, the cottage was made darker. When night comes in the last act the light from the fire was the main illumination on stage; it's surprising how effective the long shadows and dim corners can be. We were also lucky because we could afford to hire a snow projector, which is a spotlight with a rotating disc on the front; in the dark it looks as though snow is falling heavily. But the most important part is the end, when Mrs MacRoy reveals herself as Sedna, and the Northern Lights start up. How you manage this will depend on the amount of lighting you have, but the important thing is to remember the bright colours of the *Aurora Borealis*, and try to give some feeling of their brilliance, purple and blue and red and orange. If your lights are not sufficient in number, then concentrate on having a brilliant display on a small area; you can even shine the lights at the audience.

Sound

Sound can help a lot in creating atmosphere This play is set on an island, and there will be the noise of the sea, the wind, seagulls. You can't really keep the sea noise going throughout, or it loses its effect; keep it for key moments, and then gradually fade it away. The opening is most important. As the house lights go down, bring up the sound of the waves and the wind very loud for a few seconds, just to set the scene. They will explain more than any number of notes in the programme. Apart from that, you can have the bleating of sheep every now and then, and even the occasional cock crow. The places where the gale blows are marked in the text. We also had some spooky sounds when Mrs MacRoy revealed herself as Sedna, Goddess of Winter. Read the play carefully, and you'll certainly find other ideas suggest themselves. Borrowing a tape recorder shouldn't be too hard; then it's up to your ingenuity.

Final thing (with the Author's permission)

There are always things in a play – any play, which need to be changed to suit the production. Either an actor can't get his tongue round certain words, or you just *can't* find a prop, such as the weaving loom, anywhere; or your Aunt Edna has a rabbit who's stagestruck and wants to be in the show. Most authors expect a few changes to be made during rehearsals, and won't start screaming at you from the stalls on the first night unless they're changes for the worse – and you must be the judge of that.

JOHN PHILLIPS

CHARACTERS

JAKIN	the children
RENDALL	
CARILAN	
LEM	
AUNTIE	
MRS MACROY	
A STRANGER	
SEDNA	
GOAT	

The action of the play takes place on Winter Island, somewhere off the north coast of Great Britain.

ACT ONE

Scene 1: Inside the cottage
Scene 2: Half an hour later. The shore outside
Scene 3: An hour later. Inside the cottage

ACT TWO

Scene 1: Six years later. Inside the cottage
Scene 2: A few minutes later. On the shore
Scene 3: Three days later. Inside the cottage
Scene 4: Some hours later. Inside the cottage

Note: The music for all the songs in this play appears on pp. 65–72. It gives basic rhythms and melodies for the songs, which the composer suggests the performers may vary if they wish.

ACT ONE

SCENE I

Interior of a cottage on Winter Island. There is a fireplace, a ladder leading to a loft, and, up one or two steps, a small alcove room on a higher level, visible to the audience, which contains a bedstead. A fairly large window at the back gives a view of hillside and sea.

Voices are heard offstage, cries of 'Can you take the rope?', 'Right, got it!', 'Here, pass that to me!', 'Hurry up!', etc. Sheep are bleating, poultry cackling. The sound of the sea is heard very faintly throughout, also the occasional cry of gulls.

JAKIN *bursts in, carrying on his shoulder a tin trunk, which he drops carelessly on the floor. He is a thickset boy with a round face and brown hair. He is followed by* RENDALL, *a thin, responsible-looking girl. She carries a red purse on a strap, and a bundle of household equipment, a broom, etc. All the children are somewhere between ten and sixteen in age.* CARILAN *is the youngest;* JAKIN, *the eldest. They wear shabby jeans or skirts, and sweaters.*

JAKIN: Good Lord! Is *this* the place?

RENDALL: Oh, it's not too bad. There's a loft. Carilan and I can sleep there. You boys can have this room. And that little place will just do for Auntie, if we hang a curtain across.

JAKIN: Okay. [*He runs out, calling*] Lem, hang on! I'll give you a hand!

[RENDALL *carefully hangs her red purse on a nail before she too hurries out. She reappears almost immediately, helping* CARILAN *with a wicker armchair.* CARILAN *has fair, curly hair and a permanently discontented expression.*]

CARILAN: Ugh! Is this where we have to live? It's horrible! Freezing! There's nowhere to sit! *Why* did we have to come here? I know I'm going to hate it!

RENDALL: Hush!

[*She gestures to door where* AUNTIE *is just entering.* AUNTIE *is a thin, elderly, distraught-looking woman, who wears numerous cardigans, wrappers and dangling scarves, and carries various odd little cloth, string and paper bags; she wanders about, peering vaguely, without seeming to register much of what she sees.*]

RENDALL: [*continuing in a low voice*]: You *know* you thought it would be fun to live on an island. Think how lovely it will be in summer with the sea right outside.

AUNTIE [*fanning herself*]: Oh, dear, dear, dear, what a dreadful journey! I feel as if I've been put through a wringer. How *could* you drag us all this way, Rendall? I'm sure there was no need . . .

RENDALL [*gently*]: Just sit down and rest yourself, Auntie, you'll soon feel better. Carilan, can't you collect some sticks and make a fire?

CARILAN: Oh, *must* I?

[*She goes out slowly.* AUNTIE *sniffs at various bottles which she takes out of her bags; rubs stuff on her temples and wrists; swallows pills.* RENDALL *runs in and out, bringing holdalls, a box of crockery, bundles of blankets and sleeping-bags. While* RENDALL *is out of the room,* AUNTIE, *noticing the red purse, quickly and furtively snatches it and pops it into one of her bags.* RENDALL, *returning, does not notice it has gone.*]

CARILAN [*helplessly, coming in*]: I can't find any wood.

RENDALL [*patiently*]: There's lots of driftwood on the shore.

CARILAN [*whining*]: I'm so tired!

RENDALL: Oh, heavens! All right, I'll get some. Here [*handing her the kettle*] you fill the kettle in the stream then, and we'll make some tea [*encouragingly*]. [*She runs out.*]

CARILAN [*letting kettle fall back into box*]: Auntie, why do we have to stop here?

[*She goes to stand by* AUNTIE, *who puts her arm round her.*]

AUNTIE: I don't know, I'm sure, dear. She and the boys didn't see fit to consult *me*. I'm only your poor old aunt, who's brought you up from babies. Nobody cares if I have to leave my nice house and move to a desert island.

CARILAN [*whine rising to wail*]: Who's going to cook the dinner? I'm hungry!

AUNTIE: I expect Rendall will, by and by, when she's suited herself giving orders to the boys.

[*She sits in the wicker chair, putting some of her bags on the floor.* CARILAN, *noticing the strap of the red purse protruding from the bag, quietly pulls it out and pockets it.* AUNTIE, *who is adjusting scarves around her neck, does not observe this. She takes* CARILAN *on her lap, and they cling together, rocking to and fro.*]

CARILAN [*tearfully*]: We shan't really have to stop here long, shall we?

AUNTIE: Gracious, no dear. The others will get over this notion of theirs soon enough.

CARILAN: And then we'll go back where there's shops and streets?

AUNTIE: Yes, shops and streets and lovely supermarkets.

[JAKIN *and* LEM *come in,* JAKIN *with a tool-chest and fishing-rod,* LEM *with a tea-chest full of books. Slung on* LEM'*s back is a guitar, which he carefully hangs on a nail. He is thin, with a pointed face and a mop of fuzzy hair. He goes out and returns with wicker bird-basket which he puts down, even more carefully, near the window.*]

JAKIN [*to* CARILAN]: Hey, stop ducking your share of the work, you lazy little beast.

CARILAN [*outraged*]: Oh!

LEM: Yes, come on, Carilan. Even the ferrywoman's lent a hand – and all you do is sit in Auntie's lap –

JAKIN: Like a miserable, whining baby –

[RENDALL *comes in with an armful of wood which she puts in the fireplace.*]

AUNTIE: Now then, boys, Carilan's only a baby, remember, nothing like so big as you.

[LEM *shrugs and continues to go in and out with bundles.*]

JAKIN: Baby, my foot. You didn't call *me* a baby when I was her age!

RENDALL [*trying to light fire*]: Oh, bother!

AUNTIE: Carilan's the youngest; you ought to be nice to her.

CARILAN [*triumphantly*]: See!

[*Exasperatedly,* JAKIN *takes a threatening step towards* CARILAN, *who cringes back against* AUNTIE. *But at this moment,* JAKIN *is distracted by* RENDALL'*s struggle with the fire.*]

JAKIN: Here, *you're* no good. Better let me do that.

RENDALL: Thanks, Jake. I'll just –

[*She lifts the kettle, finds it empty, is on the point of snapping at* CARILAN, *but shrugs, goes out, and returns with full kettle which she puts on the hob.* AUNTIE *has taken a book from the tea-chest and is reading* sotto voce *to* CARILAN.]

LEM [*coming in with a spade and a feather mattress*]: Where's Auntie sleeping?

JAKIN: Up there in the little room.

[AUNTIE *looks round.*]

LEM [*dumping mattress on bedstead in alcove*]: There you are, Auntie. [*Goes out again.*]

AUNTIE [*absently*]: Thank you, dear.

[*She pushes off the reluctant* CARILAN, *goes into the alcove, and starts pottering about, smoothing the bed, taking things out of tin trunk, etc.* CARILAN *settles herself in the wicker armchair, continuing to read; then her attention is attracted by one of* AUNTIE'*s bags, which she has left by the chair.*]

LEM [*coming in with driftwood planks*]: I say, Jake, we can easily make some shelves and tables with these. Where's the hammer?

[JAKIN *pauses from blowing fire and passes hammer.* LEM *bangs three legs into holes in a short plank and makes a stool.*]

JAKIN [*surprised*]: Hey, that's not bad! Give back the hammer.

[*The fire is now burning, so* JAKIN *makes a table by a similar process while* LEM *makes another stool; then the two boys put planks on boxes or bricks against the wall for shelves. On these they place books and crockery.* JAKIN *strings curtain wire across window and alcove. Meanwhile* CARILAN *has found a small black notebook in another of* AUNTIE'*s bags, pulled it out, and is reading it absorbedly.*]

RENDALL [*coming in with a pail of milk*]: Isn't it lucky I learned to milk on that farm last summer? [*Seeing furniture*] Oh, I say, that looks marvellous! Here, try these.

[*She pulls some curtains out of a bundle.* LEM *and* JAKIN *hang them at the window and alcove opening, half pulled back.*]

There, Auntie! Now you've got a dear little room all to yourself!

AUNTIE [*fretfully*]: When do I get a cup of tea? That's what I want to know. Isn't that kettle boiling yet?

LEM [*looking out of the window as he hangs the curtains*]: Hey, drop everything. One of the goats is eating my seed potatoes!

[LEM, JAKIN, *and* RENDALL *run out.*]

AUNTIE [*coming out of alcove*]: Make a pot of tea, Carilan, dearie, will you? Poor old Auntie's just parched for a nice cuppa!

CARILAN [*starts guiltily and stuffs the little black book into her pocket*]: I don't know how, Auntie!

AUNTIE: Yes, you do, dear. You've often watched Rendall. Just put the tea in the pot and pour on boiling water.

CARILAN: Just a minute. [*She picks up hammer, and goes up ladder to loft and starts hammering out of sight.*]

[JAKIN *and* LEM *come in, followed by* RENDALL, *head turned, looking back.*]

RENDALL: Won't you come and have a cup of tea, Mrs MacRoy, before you go back?

[RENDALL *is followed by the ferrywoman,* MRS MACROY. *A tall figure in a long-skirted dress of dark plaid, she wears a voluminous black knitted shawl over her head, pulled forward so as almost to cover her face. She stands waiting on the threshold.* RENDALL *pours tea into the mugs which* JAKIN *sets out on the table.*]

MRS MACROY: I thank you, no. I will be taking my fee and going home before the darkness comes.

RENDALL: Oh, I hadn't thought of that. Yes, I suppose it will be dark before long.

[*They all glance at the window.*]

Thirty shillings, you said?

[MRS MACROY *inclines her head.* RENDALL *goes over to where she hung the purse and finds it gone.*]

RENDALL: That's funny. I thought I hung my purse there. Lem, did you move it when you put up your guitar?

LEM: No, of course not! Perhaps it's fallen down.

[*He and* RENDALL *search.*]

JAKIN: Sure that's where you put it?

RENDALL [*worried*]: Yes, almost sure . . . [*Glances at* AUNTIE, *who is taking no notice.*] Auntie, you haven't seen my red purse, have you? I had the exact ferry fee in it, and that's all the money we had left.

AUNTIE [*quite carefree, drinking tea.*] No, dear.

[RENDALL *looks at her in a troubled way, then at* JAKIN, *who shrugs.*]

RENDALL [*calls*]: Carilan!

CARILAN [*coming to the loft doorway with the injured air of one interrupted in an important task*]: Yes, what? I was just arranging our room.

JAKIN [*curtly*]: Have you seen Rendall's red purse?

CARILAN [*affronted*]: No, of course I haven't! Why pick on me? *I'm* not a thief! If you think somebody's taken it, why not ask –

RENDALL: All right, never mind –

JAKIN [*simultaneously with* RENDALL]: Shut up, Carilan. No one said you'd taken it. I only asked if you'd seen it.

CARILAN [*sulkily*]: Well, I haven't.

JAKIN: Better help hunt for it, then.

[*They all search except* AUNTIE, *who calmly drinks her tea, and* MRS MACROY. RENDALL *goes immediately to the bag where* AUNTIE *had put the purse; she is very much surprised not to find it there.*]

AUNTIE [*socially*]: Have you always lived in this part of the world, Mrs Thingummy?

MRS MACROY: Aye, I have that.

JAKIN: Then you must know all about this island. Why it was for sale so cheap, I mean.

MRS MACROY: Och, there was nobody just very anxious to live here.

LEM: Why? Who was the last owner? What happened to him?

MRS MACROY: He went away . . .

AUNTIE: Shopping, probably.

CARILAN [*nervously*]: But is the island really haunted? By – a ghost, or something?

MRS MACROY [*after a pause*]: There is no ghost.

[*They have all been motionless; now they start searching for the purse again.*]

But there is a legend. It is said the island belongs to winter – that every seventh year, when a very hard winter comes, the island will vanish for six months, vanish clean away and not be visible at all.

JAKIN: But – but that's silly! I mean – you can see it from the mainland, quite easily. You must be able to see it in winter –

[MRS MACROY *turns towards him. His voice dies away.*]

LEM [*quietly*]: Why does it vanish? Where does it go?

CARILAN [*frantic*]: I said this was a horrible place! We can't stay here!

JAKIN: Oh, don't be stupid, Carilan. Where else could we go?

RENDALL [*distressed*]: I'm most *terribly* sorry, Mrs MacRoy – I can't think what's happened to the purse.

LEM: I don't understand about winter. Why should the island belong to winter?

MRS MACROY: Do ye know what winter is?

JAKIN: Why, of course. Winter is when it's cold.

RENDALL: And dark. [*Glances towards window.*]

MRS MACROY: Aye, cold and dark. For six months, it will be like that. And what then?

LEM: Spring comes. Winter goes.

MRS MACROY: So! Winter goes. But *where* does winter go?

JAKIN: Back to the North Pole. No – to Australia. Places south of the equator.

MRS MACROY: So the shadow of winter will always be somewhere. And maybe there will be places that are in the shadow more than others.

LEM: And you mean this island – Winter Island – is like that? Left over from winter?

MRS MACROY: Aye, left over. An outpost on the frontier betwixt winter and summer – or maybe a buttress, a fortification. If there were not spots like this island about the globe, maybe winter would overflow entirely and flood the whole world with cold and dark.

[*There is a pause, while they all think about what she has said.*]

JAKIN: It all sounds like rubbish! As Carilan said, we *bought* the island. We paid for it with the last of Auntie's money –

MRS MACROY: Ye bought it very cheap, I am thinking ye just now said?

RENDALL: Yes, because nobody wanted it –

MRS MACROY: Maybe what ye paid will not have been the full price, but only a few years' rent – until the next Winterthing.

LEM: *Winterthing?* What's that?

MRS MACROY: That is the time when the forces of winter return to the island and hold sway over it and the island vanishes from the sight of men.

CARILAN [*whimpering*]: I don't *want* to live here!

JAKIN [*simultaneously with* CARILAN]: That *must* be nonsense, you know! Oh, do shut up, Carilan!

LEM: When is the next Winterthing due?

MRS MACROY: Six years lies between you and the Winterthing: two years to plant, two years to grow, two years to harvest . . .

JAKIN: Oh, well, six years! I'm going to build a dynamo – power from the wind. We'll have electric light and heat for the winter. But anyway, we'll all be grown up and gone long before six years are over.

MRS MACROY: Will ye so? [*There is another silence.*] And my fee? How will ye be paying that?

RENDALL [*uncomfortably*]: Well – it's a bit awkward, but perhaps I'd better explain . . .

[*The boys scowl and stare at their feet;* CARILAN *listens avidly.*]

Here, you lot, why don't you go and make sure there's nothing we've left in Mrs MacRoy's boat?

JAKIN: Oh, all right. Come on, Lem.

CARILAN: I'm not going out in the cold again!

RENDALL: Oh – go and finish tidying upstairs then.

[LEM, JAKIN, *and* CARILAN *leave.* MRS MACROY *stands motionless while* RENDALL *fidgets about.*]

RENDALL: You see – it's like this. Our aunt has brought us all up since we were babies. Our parents died in a plane crash, and we can't remember them –

[*She pauses.* MRS MACROY *says nothing.*]

RENDALL: Auntie has always been very kind to us, but – especially the last few years – she has been getting a bit *queer*. She – has this habit – you see – she can't seem to resist *taking* things. From supermarkets, you know, and – and shops. She takes dozens of things she doesn't need at all – coal scuttles, and cushions, and curling-tongs –

[*She pauses again, looking at* MRS MACROY *for sympathy.* MRS MACROY *remains impassive.*]

RENDALL: She doesn't *mean* to be wicked. Just lately, she's started an even *worse* habit. [*Pause*] She – she sets fires to buildings. Oh, not buildings with people in them, but post offices at night, or cinemas when they're empty, or football stadiums. She's mad about football stadiums. I suppose they burn very easily. So we saw the advertisement for Winter Island in *The Times*, and we decided to buy it with the last of Auntie's money and come to live up here where she's out of harm's way.

JAKIN [*bursting in*]: Come on! We've got Mrs MacRoy's boat launched, and the tide's just on the turn.

RENDALL: I was just telling Mrs MacRoy that we're sure to find the money presently –

JAKIN [*cheerfully*]: Sure to be among Auntie's things.

[AUNTIE *coughs*]

And the old girl's pretty well on in years – she can't last very much longer –

RENDALL [*scandalized*]: *Jake!*

JAKIN: Well, it's true [*quietly*]. It's not that I want her to die, but let's be honest. When she does, we can all go back to the mainland – there won't be any reason to stay on here – so we can get jobs and pay you back, Mrs Mac.

MRS MACROY [*after a pause*]: Do ye promise then?

RENDALL: Yes!

MRS MACROY: Very well, I accept your promise.

LEM [*shouting from outside*]: Hurry up!

MRS MACROY: So I will see you again before the grey wolves of winter come back to swallow the sun and the moon?

JAKIN: Er – I suppose so. [*Glancing out of the window.*] Lem! Keep her off the rocks, can't you?

[*He runs out, followed by* RENDALL. MRS MACROY *stands with her back to the audience, looking about the room.*]

CARILAN [*running down the loft steps, calling softly*]: Mrs MacRoy! Mrs MacRoy!

MRS MACROY [*turning towards her*]: Aye? What is it?

CARILAN: Mrs MacRoy, will you take me with you? Will you take me back to the mainland?

MRS MACROY: And why would I be doing that, when I have not even been paid for the trip over?

CARILAN: I can pay you! Truly I can! Will you take me? *Please!*

[*She is holding the red purse and little black notebook, very excited.*]

MRS MACROY: Och, no. I'll take all; or *none*. [*She turns on her heel and goes out swiftly.*]

CARILAN: Damn! Damn the beastly old hag! [*She clenches her fists, then goes up to the loft.*]

AUNTIE [*coming from alcove, looking through the window*]: Dear, dear! What's all the commotion? Mrs MacRoy leaving? Well, I should think she might have waited to say goodbye! Not very polite!

[*She goes out without noticing* CARILAN. *There are shouts of 'Fend her off!', 'Goodbye!', etc., from outside,* CARILAN, *suddenly galvanized by an idea, jumps up, finds a pen, and consulting the little black book, writes a few words on a bit of paper; then she goes to* LEM'*s bird basket, opens it, and takes out a white pigeon. It has a ring on its leg. She slips her paper under the ring and tosses the bird out of the window; then she takes up the book and the purse and goes upstairs once more.* AUNTIE, JAKIN, RENDALL, *and* LEM *enter.*]

JAKIN: What the dickens did the old girl mean by that grey wolves of winter bit?

RENDALL: Goodness knows!

JAKIN: At least you persuaded her to wait for her cash.

AUNTIE: I daresay there'll be a bit of supper *some* time?

JAKIN: Yes! I'm going to catch some fish.

AUNTIE: I could fancy a nice bit of fish. [*Vaguely*] Well, I shall go out till it's ready and take a look around the shops.

[*The others glance at each other uneasily; then* JAKIN *shrugs and goes out with his fishing-rod.*]

RENDALL [*worriedly*]: But, Auntie dear – don't you remember? There *aren't* any shops on this island?

AUNTIE: No *shops*?

[*She looks at* RENDALL *disbelievingly a long moment, then goes out, shaking her head.* RENDALL *sits wearily on a stool, resting her head on her hands.*]

LEM [*picking up roll of netting*]: There's quite a good pigeon-loft over the cow-byre. I'll just put Snowflake in it, to settle down; then I'll give you a hand, Rendall. Come on, Snowflake, want to stretch your wings? [*He opens the bird basket, discovers the pigeon is missing.*] *Oh!* She's gone! Snowflake's gone! *Who* can have let her out?

[RENDALL *slowly raises her head and shakes it. They are still staring at one another as the curtain falls.* CURTAIN.]

SCENE 2

A headland on the rocky shore just below the cottage. Dusk is falling; up above, the cottage is silhouetted, its windows lit up. JAKIN *and* LEM *are sitting on rocks, looking out to sea, towards the audience.* LEM *is chopping seed potatoes and putting them in boxes. He has his guitar by him; he picks it up and strums from time to time.* JAKIN *is fishing. There is the sound of waves breaking softly throughout; also the sounds of gulls crying and sheep bleating.*

JAKIN: Shame about your bird. Do you think she could have done it? Or Auntie? Or that rotten little Carilan?

LEM: It doesn't make much difference who did it – the bird's gone. She'll fly back to Bath. I just hope she get there – and that someone takes her in and gives her a good home. But there are a lot of eagles round here . . .

LEM: Auntie's wandering about up there on the hill. D'you think we ought to round her up and lead her home before she trips over a heather root?

JAKIN: Oh, she'll be all right. She can't get lost. Nothing for her to pinch, either, poor old girl. Ha! I've got a bite. [*Pulls in line, on which there is a fish.*] Two more, and that'll be one each for supper. [*Throws line back.*] One thing, we shan't be bored here. Plenty to do.

LEM [*sings*]:

> Tinker, tailor, soldier, sailor,
> All I want to be is a full-time failer;
> Rich man, poor man, beggarman, thief,
> I'd sooner be on public relief.
>
> Army, navy, medicine, law,
> Seems that in my nature there's a fatal flaw;
> Doctor, lawyer, commander-in-chief,
> What's the good of trying, I'd only come to grief.
>
> This year, next year, sometime, never,
> Failure crowns my best endeavour;
> Science, art, or literature,
> What's the good of doing it? It's all been done before.

JAKIN [*continues*]: About that thing old Mrs Mac said before she left –

LEM: Which thing?

JAKIN: The grey wolves of winter coming to swallow up the

sun. Do you suppose that was a what-chou-call-it – a figure of speech?

LEM: Yes. Or could she have meant real wolves?

JAKIN: If wolves did come to this island they'd have to swim.

LEM: No use worrying about it yet. Six years to go.

JAKIN: I wasn't worrying. [*Pause*]. I wonder what happened to the last tenant? [*Pause.*] If they are real wolves, we could set traps for them. Or shoot them. It would be rather good.

LEM: Supposing they aren't real?

JAKIN: That's stupid. If they're here at all, they must be real.

LEM: Some things can't be proved. Is a mirage real? Is your face in the glass?

JAKIN: Well, but if the island does vanish, what happens to us?

LEM: *I* don't know. Perhaps we go to sleep – hibernate, like bears. You could get some good dreams, sleeping through a whole winter.

JAKIN: Oh, *you're* no help. You won't tackle the problem sensibly.

LEM: Is it a sensible problem? [*He sings.*]

> When I was young and had no sense,
> I bought me a fiddle for eighteen pence.
> And the only song that I could sing
> Was doze in the winter and skip in the spring.

[*The song could be omitted.*]

RENDALL [*anxiously approaching them*]: Have you seen Auntie? She's been gone a long time.

JAKIN: She's roaming around somewhere. She'll be okay.

RENDALL: I'm afraid the poor old dear's bound to find it a bit strange here, a bit lonesome.

JAKIN [*pulling in another fish*]: Four! This is a small one – you can give it to Carilan.

RENDALL: I've put some potatoes on to boil.

LEM: I'm going to sleep out if it doesn't rain. [*He sings.*]

When I was young and out for kicks,
I bought me a violin for one-and-six,
But the only song that I could remember
Was dance in July and sleep in December.

[*The song could be omitted.*]

JAKIN: What's that spoilt brat doing? Nothing useful, I bet. Sometimes I really hate that girl.

RENDALL: Jake, you can't! Your own sister!

JAKIN: You can hate your own sister just as easily as anyone else. Anyway she's not a bit like me – I certainly don't feel like her brother.

RENDALL [*distressed*]: Well, you ought to! Relations ought to be fond of one another. I know Auntie has spoiled Carilan a bit –

JAKIN: A *bit!*

RENDALL: That's all the more reason why we should look after her and help her improve.

JAKIN: The only thing that would improve Carilan would be to fall off a high cliff.

LEM: Has it ever occurred to you that perhaps we *aren't* brothers and sisters?

[*They all study each others' faces.*]

RENDALL [*after a pause*]: How do you mean? I don't understand!

LEM: Well – I've been thinking about this. Can you remember Mother and Father at all?

RENDALL: No . . . No, I can't.

LEM: Jake? Can you?

JAKIN: Nope.

LEM: Nor can I. But we *ought* to be able to. Jake must have been about four when they were killed. You must have been about three, Rendall. I was two, Auntie says.

LEM: And we're awfully different from each other, our noses, our eyes, our hair, everything.

[*They compare their faces again.*]

RENDELL: What do you think, then, Lem? D'you think she adopted us from an orphans' home?

JAKIN: Fine old swindle if we're really adopted! It's one thing to come and live in this godforsaken spot to save her from being shipped off to the nuthouse if she's our proper aunt –

RENDALL: Even if she isn't our aunt, she's brought us up and cared for us. Now it's our job to look after her.

JAKIN: Oh, well. I daresay she'll have popped off before this grey-wolves-of-winter business begin.

RENDALL [*scandalized*]: Jake!

[*He shrugs.*]

CARILAN [*wanders in, sucking her finger*]: When's supper?

RENDALL: I'll start frying the fish as soon as Jake's landed this last one. They won't take a minute. Want to lay the table?

CARILAN: I'm too tired . . . Where's Auntie?

JAKIN [*playing his fish*]: Beastly little skiver.

LEM: I'll mash the spuds, shall I, Rendall?

RENDALL: Thanks, Lem. Carilan, if you want Auntie you'd better go and hunt for her, it's getting too dark anyway for her to be out wandering on her own.

CARILAN: I don't want to. I'm scared.

JAKIN [*furiously*]: Just wait till I've landed this fish!

[*He winds it in, tosses it into a basket with the others, and starts threateningly towards* CARILAN, *who retreats but comes up against a rock; he shoots out an arm and grabs her.*]

Now, look here, young Carilan! There's going to be a lot less of the Auntie's baby caper from now on, d'you hear? You're damn well going to pull your weight on the island, like the rest of us.

CARILAN: Ooh, you beast, you're hurting me! Let go!

[*She kicks his shin, he cuffs her; she breaks into loud artificial wails.*]

RENDALL: Stop it – stop it, you two! That's enough, Jake. Leave her alone. Carilan, will you *please* go and look for Auntie?

[CARILAN *moves off slowly, casting angry looks at* JAKIN.]

LEM: No need. Here she is coming down the hill. [*Pause*] What ever is she carrying?

[*They all look offstage.*]

RENDALL [*forebodingly*]: She *can't* have stolen anything? Jake, you did say you'd been all over the island, that it was quite uninhabited?

JAKIN: Sure. Our place is the only house on it.

RENDALL: Well then what –

LEM [*simultaneously with* RENDALL]: Good heavens, it's –

[AUNTIE *comes in, carefully carrying a white, shawl-wrapped bundle in her arms.*]

JAKIN [*very apprehensively*]: Auntie. What have you got there?

[AUNTIE *wanders on, without answering, to the centre of the stage.*]

CARILAN [*turning and following* AUNTIE]: Auntie, Jake's been horrible to me! He pinched my arm. *Look*, it's turning blue! And he hit me!

[AUNTIE, *absorbed in her bundle, takes no notice.*]

He pulled my hair! And he said I was a beastly little skiver! *Auntie!*

AUNTIE [*absently*]: Oh, do stop being so tiresome, Carilan. Can't you see I'm too busy to bother with you now?

CARILAN [*bursting into tears*]: *Auntie!* [*She pulls at* AUNTIE'*s arm.*]

AUNTIE [*crossly*]: Now look what you've gone and done. You've woken the baby!

JAKIN, LEM, *and* RENDALL [*together*]: *Baby?*

[*The bundle in* AUNTIE'*s arms gives the thin cry of a young baby.*]

RENDALL [*horrified*]: Auntie! You've *taken somebody's baby?* Where did you find it?

AUNTIE [*crooning over her bundle*]: Isn't she a little love then? Wuzza, wuzza, Auntie's precious! See, children, I've found you a dear little new sister. If you're very good, you can help me bathe her sometimes. There, there, my ducky wucky, don't cry then! Do you want to look at her? There's a lovely girl – Auntie's little Sedna.

LEM: Sedna?

JAKIN: How do you know her name's Sedna?

AUNTIE: Why, of course, I know! How do I *know*? Just the way I knew yours was Jakin, silly boy! Not too close, now . . .

RENDALL: But, Auntie, *where did you find her*?

AUNTIE [*vaguely*]: Oh, just along there, poor little mite . . . [*She moves towards cottage.*]

CARILAN [*catching hold of a dangling end of the shawl as* AUNTIE *moves past her*]: Auntie! Aren't you going to tell Jakin he's not to hit me?

AUNTIE [*giving* CARILAN *an absent-minded slap*]: Stop whining Carilan! Remember, you're not the youngest any more now. [*She goes out.*]

[JAKIN, LEM, *and* RENDALL *stare at one another at a loss, then slowly follow* AUNTIE. CARILAN, *left behind, stares after them for a moment; then, in a fury, picks up* JAKIN'*s basket and hurls the fish in it back into the sea.* CURTAIN.]

SCENE 3

LEM [*appears before curtain, singing*]:

Hushabye, baby,
Sucking your thumb,
Very soon, maybe,
Winter will come.

Hush, little Sedna,
Hear the wind blow;
Dream of the island
Covered in snow.

Hushabye, baby,
Dream a fine dream;
Ice will be forming
Over the stream;

Fish will be sleeping
Under the ice.
Hushabye, baby,
That's my advice.

Hibernate, baby,
Slumber and learn;
Sooner or later,
Spring will return.

[*While* LEM *is singing, the curtain rises to reveal the interior of the cottage, lit by candles. The fire burns bright.* RENDALL *is making a wool-on-canvas rug.* CARILAN *sits sulkily by the fire.* AUNTIE'*s silhouette is seen on the curtain of the alcove, moving about. The kettle is steaming on the hob. The sound of the wind soughing can be heard from time to time.*]

AUNTIE [*putting her head around the curtain*]: All right, you can stop now, Lem. She's settling nicely. [*Head withdrawn again.*]

LEM [*laying down his guitar, beginning to dry a few dishes by washing-up bowl on table*]: When d'you suppose Jake will be back?

RENDALL: He said he might set a few night lines. He was still angry about the fish. [CARILAN *ostentatiously turns her back.*]

LEM: You can hardly blame him. Nothing but spuds for supper after all his work.

CARILAN [*loudly*]: He shouldn't have hit me and called me names.

RENDALL: You're still in disgrace, Carilan; we aren't speaking to you. You'd better go to bed.

CARILAN: If you aren't speaking to me, you can't send me to bed. Anyway, you've no right!

LEM: Stay up, then; nobody cares, one way or the other.

[CARILAN, *shoulders hunched, stares at fire.*]

JAKIN [*comes in wearing oilskins*]: Raining hard now, and the wind's getting up; too rough for night lines.

[*The baby whimpers behind the alcove curtains;* AUNTIE'*s voice is heard hushing her.*]

RENDALL: What are we going to do about the baby?

JAKIN: Soon as Lem and I have built the boat, we'll row over and discover if she belongs to anyone on the mainland.

RENDALL: Do you think she could be Mrs MacRoy's?

JAKIN: Use your nut, Rendall! Mrs Mac's far too old to have a baby.

RENDALL: That's true . . .

LEM: Mrs MacRoy wouldn't have left her on thc island.

RENDALL: I shouldn't have thought *anybody* would leave her. But she was here . . .

JAKIN: Tell you what – I bet that's how Auntie collected *us*; she pinched us.

RENDALL: Oh, how awful! You mean, you think she *stole* us?

JAKIN: Right! Out of prams, I daresay, when they were parked outside Woolworth's. Wouldn't I just be pleased to prove that I'm not Carilan's brother!

CARILAN: Oh, charming! No gladder than I am to know I'm not your sister, you great boring bully!

[JAKIN *starts towards her angrily; she nips up the steps to the loft and pulls the curtain across the door.*]

RENDALL [*wearily*]: Leave her alone, Jake. We've enough to worry about without you two quarrelling all the time.

AUNTIE [*coming out with an empty hot-water bottle*]: Give us a drop of hot water in this, Rendall, would you? The poor angel's got a bit of wind in her precious tumtum.

[RENDALL *fills the bottle from the kettle.*]

JAKIN: Auntie?

AUNTIE [*absently*]: Yes, dear . . .

JAKIN: When Rendall and Lem and I were babies, did you kidnap us the way you've just brought in this baby?

AUNTIE [*vaguely*]: What, dear? It's not too hot, is it Rendall?

JAKIN [*loudly*]: Did you steal us out of our prams?

AUNTIE [*testing*]: That's fine. Wheel you out in your prams? Certainly I did – every day that was fine enough. I believe in fresh air for babies.

JAKIN: Did you *steal* us?

AUNTIE: Don't bother me now, like a good boy. Can't you see I'm busy and distracted? Eh, dear, gracious knows what gets into them, and me all flummoxed and flustered over that little treasure in there . . . [*Shaking her head distractedly, she takes the bottle from* RENDALL *and returns to the alcove.*]

LEM: It's no use. You'll never get a sensible answer out of her [*pause.*] Hark to the wind.

[*They all listen; the wind has risen to gale force, and a wave breaks thunderously on the shore.*]

Did you hear Mrs MacRoy, on the way over, saying that when there's a gale up here, it oftens lasts for six weeks or more? From the sound, I shouldn't wonder if we weren't in for one of those six weeks' affairs. On our first night, too.

JAKIN: Reckon you're right. We'd better go and make sure the animals are okay.

[*Both boys go out.*]

AUNTIE [*emerging from the alcove*]: Harken to it roar! One thing, the storm doesn't disturb her a bit. Sleeping like an angel, bless her. Make me a drink of Horlicks, Rendall, like a good girl.

RENDALL [*putting a pan on the fire*]: There's no Horlicks, I'm afraid, Auntie; you'll have to make do with milk.

AUNTIE [*peevishly*]: Haven't you any Horlicks? Eh, dear, dear! Milk's not nearly so digestible on its own. [*She sits in the wicker armchair, muttering.*] Mercy on us, what a place to live.

RENDALL: Auntie. [*Pause.*] Auntie!

AUNTIE: Eh? What, then?

RENDALL [*quietly but intensely*]: Auntie, it is true what Jake said? That you stole us out of our prams?

AUNTIE: *You* bothering me about that now, too? Can't I have any peace?

RENDALL: No, but *is* it true, Auntie? Did you take us from different people when we were babies?

AUNTIE [*vaguely*] Babies . . . outside the fish market was a good place, people didn't like to take babies in there.

Once, it was a pram with a coat-of-arms and a Brussels lace shawl . . .

RENDALL: Auntie! What do you mean?

AUNTIE [*after a long pause, piteously*]: It's no use. It's no use your bothering me. I just can't remember. I'm too old, too old, I tell you!

[*She comes to a halt and stares at* RENDALL; *her head has developed the tremor of old age. After gazing at her hopelessly for a moment,* RENDALL *crosses to her, kneels, and puts her arms round* AUNTIE'*s waist. Staring ahead,* AUNTIE *accepts the embrace without returning it. The noise of the wind outside rises to such a howl that it might almost be that of wolves.* CURTAIN.]

ACT TWO

SCENE I

LEM [*appears before curtain, singing*]:

Remember how a house
  Reminds you how a tree
Reminds you how it always
  Used to be?

Remember how a word
  Reminds you how a rhyme
Recalls a thought of once
  Upon a time?

Remember how a smile
  Reminds you how a face
Reminds you of some distant
  Other place?

Remember how the sun
  Reminds you how the snow
Reminds you how it all was
  Long ago?

[*During the song, the curtain rises on the interior of the cottage. There are some additions: a loom with a half-finished web; a homemade radio on the shelf; an electric-light bulb dangling on cord; bits of homemade pottery; a telescope on a stand by the window, barrels of apples. All the characters except* AUNTIE *are now wearing shaggy homemade sweaters and garments of handwoven cloth.* RENDALL *is sitting by the fireside, finishing off a jersey.*]

LEM [*puts down the guitar, crosses to the homemade calendar on the wall, and strikes out a square*]: Do you realize what day this is?

RENDALL: Sedna's birthday – the day we found her. I've just got this finished in time. [*Shakes out jersey she has completed.*]

LEM: We've been here six years.

RENDALL: I know – and I'm getting scared, Lem. What's going to happen to us?

LEM: Winterthing's coming, I suppose. It's lucky Jake managed to get the dynamo to work before he got bored with it.

RENDALL [*sceptically*]: If that doesn't break down, it'll be about the only thing that *does* work.

RENDALL: Six years, and we still haven't got across to the mainland. Lem, I'm so worried about Mrs MacRoy's feel Do you think she'll be very angry? It's just the way she said; nothing here has turned out how we expected. Somehow I never thought we'd really have to stay six years –

LEM: You thought Auntie would die, you mean?

RENDALL: Well – yes – I suppose so. After all, *think* how old she must be by now. And yet she doesn't look any older.

LEM: None of us do. Except for Sedna.

RENDALL: And she grows, but she doesn't really change. Why do you suppose she doesn't learn to talk?

LEM: Maybe she doesn't want to. Maybe she feels it isn't worth while . . .

RENDALL: Sometimes I feel as if we were all just waiting – no, as if the *island* were waiting.

LEM: What for?

RENDALL: For winter, I suppose.

LEM: In the book I'm reading now it says that long ago people used to light bonfires to try and stop winter coming.

RENDALL: Did they stop it?

LEM: I don't think so . . . But I don't want to stop the Winterthing. I want to see what happens.

RENDALL: It frightens me. If the sun and moon vanish? Think how dark it would be . . .

LEM: We've got our dynamo – perhaps. And tallow candles. Anyway, dark's not so bad. [*He sings.*]

Dark is soft, like fur,
Velvet, like a purr,
Lies warm, lies close,
On fingers and toes.

[*While* LEM *sings,* SEDNA *enters. She is now apparently about six years old. She has long dark hair, and she is wearing a handwoven black and white checked dress. Her feet are bare. She carries the white shawl in which she was first wrapped; it is now very grubby. She rubs one end against her cheek, while trailing the other along the ground; she sucks her thumb most of the time.*]

RENDALL: Hullo, lovey.

[*As* SEDNA *moves by,* RENDALL *gives her an affectionate hug and slips the new jersey over her head.* SEDNA *does not smile or speak, but seems solemnly pleased. She wanders on and settles in what is evidently an accustomed position, leaning against* LEM; *he rumples her hair.*]

LEM: [*sings*]:

If dark cost money,
Rich people only
Would be able to pay
And rest them from day.

If dark were not given
Each night from heaven,
On field and town and park
Men would have to make dark.

Dark is so warm, so deep.
Without dark, how could we sleep?

AUNTIE [*enters from above, yawning fretfully*]: Do you have to kick up such a racket, Lem? You woke me from my afternoon nap.

LEM: Sorry, Auntie. [*He takes a string from his pocket and starts playing cat's-cradle with* SEDNA.]

AUNTIE: Isn't it nearly time for a cup of herb tea?

RENDALL [*sighing, but good-naturedly*]: I expect so. It usually is. [*Puts kettle on.*]

LEM [*to* SEDNA]: What have you done with your necklace, little 'un? Left it outside?

[*She shakes her head.*]

Never mind; I'll have a look for it presently.

[AUNTIE *crosses to the radio and turns it on. There are a few words of weather forecast; then a blast of crackle and howl.*]

AUNTIE: I do wish we could get the Archers. Or Desert Island Discs. Or even Family Choice. Not a single bit of comfort or pleasure do I have; no neighbours to talk to, nothing to see, nowhere to go . . .

LEM: Oh, Auntie! We look after you as well as we can.

AUNTIE: Oh, I don't *starve*. [*She sits.*] Come here, Sedna dearie. Time for your talking lesson.

[SEDNA *comes obediently and sits on* AUNTIE'*s lap. She seems quite content to do so, but makes no attempt to co-operate during the instruction that follows.*]

AUNTIE: Now, say after me: Rendall – is weaving. Lem – has – his guitar. Jakin – is catching – fish. Carilan – is teasing – the goat.

[SEDNA *scowls at mention of* CARILAN.]

Your shawl's dreadful dirty, lambie. You ought to let Rendall wash it.

[SEDNA *clings closer to the shawl.*]

RENDALL: It's no good; you can't pry it away from her. [*Having made tea, she goes to the door and shouts.*] Carilan! Tea's ready! Tell Jake, will you?

[*Offstage* CARILAN'*s voice is faintly heard replying.*]

AUNTIE: The goats – are in the barn. The hens – are in the shed. The tea – is in the pot.

[RENDALL *pours tea;* CARILAN *strolls in; as soon as she enters,* SEDNA *gets off* AUNTIE'*s lap and follows her closely.*]

CARILAN [*taking tea from* RENDALL]: I can do with that; I'm parched. [*Noticing* SEDNA] Rendall, tell Sedna to stop following me around. I'm fed up with her. [*To* SEDNA] Leave me alone, will you?

RENDALL [*perplexed*]: She must have some reason for it. What have you been doing to her?

CARILAN: Nothing!

[SEDNA, *still trailing shawl, now stands in front of her, not exactly threatening, just dogged.*]

RENDALL: You probably took something of hers – Yes, you have, too. You're wearing the shell necklace Lem made Sedna for her birthday.

LEM: That was a pretty mean trick, Carilan. Give it back.

AUNTIE: It's naughty to take Sedna's things, Carilan, you're not to do it! Poor little lamb, did nasty unkind Carilan take her shells?

CARILAN [*sulkily*]: It was only a joke. Anyway she's just a baby, she doesn't care.

LEM: She does care.

RENDALL: And she's not such a baby as all that. At the rate she's growing, she'll soon be as big as you.

[*Somewhat startled by this suggestion,* CARILAN *takes off the shell necklace and reluctantly returns it to* SEDNA, *who stands waiting, motionless. Along with the necklace,* CARILAN *administers a surreptitious pinch;* SEDNA *winces, but does not cry.*]

RENDALL: Did you tell Jake tea was ready?

CARILAN: He was too far off. He'll come of his own accord soon, I daresay.

RENDALL [*exasperated*]: Oh, Carilan! [*Goes out.*]

LEM: If I were you, I'd be a bit kinder to Sedna.

CARILAN: Well you aren't me, so keep your goody-goody opinions to yourself.

LEM: One of these days you're going to be really sorry.

CARILAN: Oh, nuts to you, know-all! What use are *you*? You can't even help Jake with his dynamo; all you can do is read, read, and grow potatoes. I'm going upstairs. [*She takes her cup of tea up to the loft, making a face at* SEDNA *as she passes.*]

AUNTIE [*yawning*]: Eh, dear, dear, I wonder why children turn so nasty and quarrelsome once they leave off being babies. I wish you were all babies again. That I do!

LEM: I'm sure you do, Auntie.

AUNTIE: I think I'll go back to bed and have a little doze till suppertime; there's no other way to amuse oneself in this miserable place. [*Retires to alcove.*]

[SEDNA *curls up again beside* LEM.]

LEM [*sings softly*]:

> Dark is soft, like fur,
> Velvet, like a purr.
> Lies warm, lies close,
> On fingers and toes.
>
> Dark is so warm, so deep,
> Without dark, how could we sleep?

[JAKIN *comes in. He has changed more than the others; not physically, but he looks as if he has given up caring about anything. His clothes are untidy, his hair shaggy. He slouches in and throws himself into a chair.*]

LEM: Any fish?

JAKIN: Three or four; someone'll have to manage without. I didn't go all the way around. Couldn't be bothered. It's getting terribly cold.

LEM: Want some tea?

JAKIN: Pour me a cup, will you? I can't reach from here. [*Accepts cup from* LEM, *drinks a little, then puts it on the floor.*] I'm fed up!

LEM: With what?

JAKIN: Everything! The boat's bottom boards have gone again, just when I thought I had them fixed; the windmill's conked; and any minute now the dynamo will, too. I can tell you, I'm not staying here through this Winterthing without electricity!

LEM: How do you mean? What will you do?

JAKIN: When old Mrs MacRoy comes over for her thirty bob – I shall hitch a ride back with her.

LEM [*rather shocked*]: And leave us to look after Auntie?

JAKIN: Anyone who wants can come too – Auntie included.

LEM: If Auntie went back, she'd do something awful and get sent to an asylum.

JAKIN: So what? Maybe it would have been better if she'd been put away in the first place.

LEM: I don't know what Rendall will say –

JAKIN: I do! Moan, moan, moan! Rendall's always fussing over Auntie, and Auntie's always fussing over Sedna, and Carilan's always fussing over herself, selfish little beast –

CARILAN [*emerging from loft, starting down steps*]: Thanks! Thanks very much!

JAKIN: Oh rats. If you're coming down, I'm off. [*He goes.*]

LEM [*Calling after him*]: Hey, Jake! Did you feed the goat? [LEM *follows* JAKIN *out.*]

[SEDNA *remains curled up inconspicuously against bench.* CARILAN, *not noticing her, sees* AUNTIE'*s bag left hanging over chair-back and begins rummaging in it. Meanwhile* SEDNA *gets up silently, comes and stands by* CARILAN *watching her steadily;* CARILAN *suddenly becomes aware of her, and gives a violent start.*]

CARILAN: What do *you* want?

[SEDNA *looks at her in silence.*]

You think you're so wonderful, don't you? Dear little Sedna, with her talking lessons, and her shell necklace, and her birthday sweater, and her precious shawl – *ugh!*

[*She makes a hideous face at* SEDNA, *putting out her tongue;* SEDNA *stares back impassively.*]

D'you want to know what *I* think of you? I think you're a rotten little sneaking, spying toad, and I wouldn't care a bit if you fell in the sea and got drowned. Not a bit! But you look pretty silly. I can tell you, acting like a two-year-old, dragging that shawl about and sucking your thumb! [*With a sudden whisk she snatches away* SEDNA'*s shawl and stuffs it into the fire, where it immediately blazes up.*] There! That's the end of *that*!

[SEDNA *makes a startled movement, opens her mouth, shudders as the shawl burns, but does not speak;* CARILAN *pokes it down until it is all gone, then grins at* SEDNA.]

Now go and cry to your precious Lem!

[RENDALL *puts head round door.*]

RENDALL: Hey, where is everybody? Listen, I'm almost sure there's a sail, over there to the east –

CARILAN: Mrs MacRoy's boat?

RENDALL: No, looks like a yacht – where are the boys?

CARILAN: Outside somewhere –

[RENDALL *runs out again, after a moment's hesitation,* CARILAN *follows. Left alone,* SEDNA *stand still and draws herself up so she appears to be taller. Moving slowly, she goes to fireplace and brings out a black shawl which she drapes over head and shoulders. From now on she is invisible to people onstage.*]

LEM [*runs in, calling over his shoulder*]: Sedna! Sedna! [*He looks around in surprise, expecting to find* SEDNA; *then he takes the telescope off its stand.* AUNTIE *pokes her head through the curtain.*] Where's Sedna, Auntie? I thought she might like to come and see the yacht.

AUNTIE: Yacht, what yacht?

LEM: There's a yacht, a sailing ship, coming down the channel. [*Calling up the loft stairs.*] Sedna! Where can she be?

AUNTIE: I expect she went out [*Sniffs.*]

LEM: Queer I didn't notice her. I suppose I had my eyes on the sea.

AUNTIE: Let's go and see this boat then.

LEM: Put on something warm if you're coming out, Auntie, it's starting to snow.

[*As* LEM *runs out again,* AUNTIE *returns to the alcove and puts on an elderly imitation astrakhan coat, then starts to follow.*]

AUNTIE: Snow in the summer! I ask you, what a climate! And I suppose little Sedna's gone running out barefoot. Eh, dear, dear, what a worry children are when they get to the running-about age! Well, let's have a look at this yacht; maybe the man would take some of us over to the mainland. No harm in asking.

[*Not seeing* SEDNA, *who stands motionless, midstage,* AUNTIE *passes close to her and goes out.*

CURTAIN.]

SCENE 2

The shore. Dusk; occasional flakes of snow. RENDALL *and* CARILAN *stand shivering, staring along the shore.* JAKIN*'s and* LEM*'s voices, offstage, come from the direction in which the girls are looking.*

JAKIN [*off*]: Looks as if he's making this way.
LEM [*off*]: I believe he's in trouble.
JAKIN [*off*]: Better get something we can use as fenders in case he wants to tie up –

[SEDNA, *wearing her black shawl, comes in and stands among them; they do not see her.*]

AUNTIE: I wonder where Sedna can have got to? She'd like to see this boat, I expect. Look, you can see the man's face quite plain now –
RENDALL: He's letting down his sail.
CARILAN: Look, he's thrown a rope; Jake's caught it. There's letters on the boat – *P, R, E, T* ...
RENDALL: It's the boat's name – *Pretty Rogue* – I bet that poor man's frozen and hungry – I'll put some soup on – [*She runs out.*]
AUNTIE: Rendall! Rendall! Mind you put out the best tablecloth and the gilt-edged bowls – Bother the girl, she doesn't hear me! [*She goes out after* RENDALL, *muttering*] Such a long time since we entertained ...

[JAKIN *and* LEM *come in with the* STRANGER, *who is dressed in oilskins and has a short black beard.* LEM *carries the telescope.*]

STRANGER: I got blown off course, you see – chart went overboard –
JAKIN: Where were you making for?
STRANGER: Crossing to Ireland.
LEM: Ireland! You certainly were off course. But we've a map that might help.
JAKIN: You'd better stay here tonight; go on tomorrow.
STRANGER: Oh, thanks, but I'd better get on. I've an appointment with a fellow on the other side, and he'll be

wondering what's happened to me as it is. We run a little line in cut-price goods, you see –

JAKIN: Smuggling?

STRANGER [*winking*]: Least said, soonest mended. Those as asks no questions get to hear no lies. But I'd certainly be grateful for a meal, and a fill-up of my water barrel, and if you had a spare bit of rope – one of my halyards went in the last blow, and I'm a bit short –

LEM: I'll get the map and a rope –

JAKIN: I'll fill the water barrel.

[*He and* LEM *run out.*]

CARILAN: Listen! [*She grabs the stranger's arm.*] Will you take me away from here?

STRANGER: Take you away?

CARILAN: Yes! To Ireland, or wherever you are going.

STRANGER [*very doubtfully*]: Oh, I dunno about that. Take you away? Why?

CARILAN: Oh, please! Look, I can pay you! I'll pay you thirty shillings; it's all I have. Here, take it, quick! [*She pulls the red purse out of her pocket and pushes it into his hand.*] Do, please take me. I expect you'll get a reward, too. Lord Ullswater is my father; he'll probably pay you something when he hears you've rescued me.

STRANGER [*sceptically*]: Rescued you? Why, you been kidnapped, or something.

CARILAN: Yes, when I was a baby! *Will* you take me?

STRANGER [*has been holding the purse doubtfully; now pockets it.*]: Eh, now, that does seem to ring a bell. Ullswater baby stolen from pram . . . But that was a long time ago, surely, years ago? You ought to be older.

CARILAN [*impatiently*]: Oh, that's this place; nobody seems to grow older here.

STRANGER: You're not kidding? Where is this place, then?

CARILAN: Winter Island.

STRANGER: *Winter Island?* The spot that vanishes clean away every seventh year? Hey, I'm getting out of here. Why didn't somebody *tell* me?

CARILAN: But you'll take me with you? Please, please!

[JAKIN *and* LEM *come in with rope, water barrel, etc.*]

STRANGER [*to* CARILAN]: Oh, all right, if you can be ready in not more than five minutes.

[CARILAN *claps her hands and darts out.*]

JAKIN: I'll put the barrel on board. [*Runs out.*]

LEM [*showing map*]: Look, this is where we are. Winter Island –

STRANGER: Yes, so the girl just told me. I'm not stopping here! Thanks for the things. and I'll be right on my way.

LEM: Won't you even wait for a meal? My sister's hotting up some soup–

STRANGER: Ta, but I don't fancy hanging about on a haunted island.

LEM [*shrugging*]: Suit yourself. Have you a flask? She could put some soup in that.

STRANGER: Yeah, thanks. In the cabin you'll see it – a big red one.

[LEM *goes out.*]

Winter Island, eh? Just my luck.

JAKIN [*returning*] Here's the rope. [*Looking both ways.*] Hey, mister! When you go, will you take me with you? I'll work my passage – I won't be any trouble.

STRANGER: Sorry, mate – no room.

JAKIN: Oh, please! I'm so fed up with living on this rotten island. I'll get a job as soon as I land on the other side and pay you back – honest!

STRANGER: Sorry, but can't be done.

AUNTIE [*coming in*]: How do you do! Pleased to meet you! Nasty cold weather we're having! Won't you come up to the house? My nieces are just preparing a meal.

JAKIN: Oh – this is my aunt. [*He hesitates over the word 'aunt'.*]

STRANGER: Sorry, ma'am, but can't stay. Kind of you, but I must be on my way. Thanks all the same.

AUNTIE: Can't *stay*? You've come all the way here, and you only stop five minutes? You must be joking? You can stay the night, surely?

STRANGER: Very sorry.

AUNTIE: Well – it seems most peculiar to me to come to a place and only stay five minutes. But if you really have to go, perhaps you'd be good enough to ferry me over to the mainland.

STRANGER: I'm not going that way I'm afraid, lady. Going over to Ireland, see?

AUNTIE: It would hardly be out of your way at all.

STRANGER: Very sorry.

AUNTIE: Then could you take me to Ireland?

STRANGER: Look here, what *is* all this? You all got the plague or something?

AUNTIE: I should be very much obliged if you would take me. It would be no extra trouble to you.

STRANGER: Now, look – I'm very sorry, but I am not the Stranraer ferry. Understand? I'm not taking on any more passengers. And I am leaving *now*.

AUNTIE [*dazedly*]: You *won't* take me? You mean you won't *take* me?

RENDALL [*coming in with a vacuum flask of soup*]: Sorry you can't stay, but maybe you're wise. It's coming up very cold and blowy; fog, too. You can't see the mainland. You might get cut off here . . . What's the matter, Auntie? Why are you crying?

AUNTIE: He won't take me! He won't take me away!

RENDALL: Oh, dear, I was afraid something like this might happen. [*She hands the flask to the* STRANGER *and puts her arms round* AUNTIE *who has sat down on a rock and is swaying to and fro.*] Auntie, you wouldn't really want to go away and leave us all, would you? [*To* STRANGER] Perhaps it would be best if you went quite quickly. Have you got all you need now?

STRANGER: Just waiting for the little girl.

RENDALL: Little girl?

[CARILAN *runs in, carrying the duffel bag. She is followed by* LEM.]

CARILAN: Right, I'm ready.

JAKIN: Do you mean he's taking *you*?

CARILAN [*triumphantly*]: He's taking me to Ireland, where I'll be able to send a message to my father.

RENDALL, JAKIN *and* LEM [*together*]: Your *father*?

RENDALL: How do you mean, your father?

JAKIN: What the dickens are you talking about?

CARILAN: My own father! I found Auntie's little black book – a long time ago – where she'd written down the addresses of the families she'd stolen us from.

[*They all gasp.*]

My father was a lord – Lord Ullswater, D'Arcy House, Bath. So now I'm going to him. See?

STRANGER: Come on, then, missie. We must be sailing.

RENDALL: Auntie!

[*But* AUNTIE *is wrapped up in her own troubles.*]

JAKIN: Hey, damn it, wait! D'you mean to say you've known all the time – where is this little black book?

CARILAN: It's going where you won't be able to get a look at it. [*Throws book into sea. Venomously.*] There! You've all been so foul to me always that it just serves you right if you never find out who your fathers and mothers are. And if you all vanish in the Winterthing and never come back I shall be *glad*. I shall just *laugh*. So goodbye!

JAKIN [*to* STRANGER]: Well, I wish you joy of her! I can tell you, if it comes on to blow, *she* won't be any use. [*Without waiting to see the embarkation, he walks off.*]

LEM: I'll cast you off.

[CARILAN, *following* STRANGER, *goes off.*]

RENDALL: Come along, Auntie; we'll go home and I'll make you a lovely cup of tea. [*She starts to lead out the sobbing* AUNTIE, *then pauses.*] Auntie, if Carilan's father was Lord Ullswater, what were the other names in your little book? Can you tell me?

AUNTIE [*wildly*]: Oh, how do I know? I don't even know what you're talking about! It's all so long ago – I can't remember. I can't remember!

[*The stage rapidly becomes darker, and the snow falls thicker.*

SEDNA *stands motionless, looking off towards place where the* Pretty Rogue *is putting to sea.* CURTAIN.]

SCENE 3

LEM [*appears before curtain, singing*]:

> If winter comes, with snow and blow,
> Can spring be far behind?
> Though clouds be grey, the wise men say,
> They must be silver-lined
> – Or if not, then never mind.
>
> Your hands will freeze, your nose, your knees,
> Your fingers all turn blue.
> Just rub them with a pinch of snow,
> There's nothing else to do
> – And I daresay we'll get through.

[*During the song the curtain rises on the interior of the cottage; snow visible outside window; electric light very dim.* RENDALL *appears from* AUNTIE'S *alcove, drawing the curtain behind her.*]

LEM: Auntie having a nap?

RENDALL: Yes, at last. She takes much longer to drop off since the boat came; just as she's getting drowsy, she starts thinking about supermarkets. [*She crosses to the radio and tries it; there is a blast of static which settles to a faint hum.*]

LEM: Is she still asking about Sedna?

RENDALL: Yes! And I don't know what to say . . . Where's Sedna gone? When's she coming back? It's hardly likely [*her voice trembles*] that we'll find Sedna somewhere now; after three days in this bitter cold. But I simply daren't tell Auntie that. I miss Sedna *dreadfully*. [*She cries a little, then wipes her eyes resolutely.*] Where's Jake?

LEM: I don't know. He seemed rather restless.

RENDALL: I wish that boat had never come here . . . [*She sits down and starts weaving.*] Is it still snowing?

LEM: A little. And the edge of the sea is starting to freeze.

[*He puts some driftwood on the fire, then takes up a book and reads.*]

LEM [*after a pause*]: Rendall.

RENDALL: Yes?

LEM: I don't think Sedna will come back.

RENDALL [*with the impatience of unhappiness*]: Isn't that what I just *said*?

LEM: I mean – I think, if she does come, that she won't be the same.

RENDALL [*uneasily, after a pause*]: I don't understand.

LEM: Listen to this. [*Reading from book.*] 'The Goddess of Winter, who is daughter of the North Wind, and Queen of Darkness, lives under the ocean. In the autumn she returns to the land, driving her team of grey wolves, who will swallow the sun and the moon. Her approach is announced by a loud knocking under the ice; sometimes, then, men light fires on the seashore in hopes of driving her away, but this is vain, for in the tug of war between winter and summer, winter is sure to triumph. She catches the sun in a net of seaweed, and with a whip of seaweed she guides the wind. Men should beware of arousing her malice, for to those who offend her she can be a pitiless enemy. Her name is Sedna.'

RENDALL: *Sedna?* The Queen of Winter?

[*The wind outside rises to a howl.*]

RENDALL: [*taking the book.*]: But . . . surely that can't be the same as *our* little Sedna? Can it?

[*While they stand looking at one another, there is a loud knocking outside, which seems to come first from one side of the cottage, then from the other.*]

RENDALL [*teeth chattering*]: What's that?

LEM: It must be Jake. [*He moves to open the door.*]

RENDALL: *Don't* – don't open it!

[*But he has already done so and looked out.*]

LEM: Nobody there . . . I believe I can see Jake coming down the hill.

[*The radio, which has been muttering, suddenly comes out loud and clear.*]

RADIO: . . . The small boat wrecked last night off Innisbalin Island has now been identified as the *Pretty Rogue* from Port Kintrae. The two people on board were both drowned. The boat ran into a small iceberg and was cut in half. It is extremely unusual for icebergs to be found so far south at this time of year . . . [*Dies out.*]

RENDALL: The *Pretty Rogue*! But that's – that was the name of the boat that –

LEM [*quickly*]: It may not be the same one –

JAKIN [*coming in covered with snow*]: One of your precious sheep is stuck on a rockface; looks likely to fall into the sea. Do you care?

RENDALL: My goodness, of course! You're sure – you're sure it's not Sedna.?

JAKIN: I do know a sheep when I see one.

LEM: Where is it?

JAKIN: Over on the west side.

RENDALL: We must go over there right away.

[RENDALL *and* LEM *hurriedly put on thick outer wear and take ropes, sticks and lanterns.* JAKIN, *meanwhile, has put a few things in a rucksack; he starts for the door.*]

RENDALL [*suddenly noticing this*]: Jake – where are you taking that stuff? Aren't you coming with us?

JAKIN [*very offhand*]: No, I'm off.

RENDALL: Off? How do you mean?

LEM: Off?

JAKIN: I reckon the channel's frozen right across. I'm going to walk over to the mainland and hitchhike down to London and get a job.

RENDALL: Jake! You can't! Walk across? You must be crazy! It's much too dangerous!

LEM: What about your dynamo?

JAKIN: I'm fed up with that, too. It's just about due to break down again.

RENDALL: Go off and leave us – just like that?

JAKIN: Go off and leave you – just like that.

RENDALL: But what about looking after Auntie? What about finding out who your parents were?

JAKIN: She's no auntie of mine. You're fond of the old trout; you look after her. And if she remembers the names – though I don't think she ever will, she's too far around the bend by now – you can send mine on a postcard. I'll let you know my London address when I have one. Goodbye now. [*He goes to door.*]

RENDALL [*starting after him, but too late to stop him*]: Jake! Suppose the ice breaks?

JAKIN: That'll be just too bad. Bye! [*He goes out.*]

LEM: Good luck, Jake.

RENDALL [*looking outside*]: He's started across . . . I can only just see – it's so dim, with the snow. Do you think he'll ever get across?

LEM: Well, there's no use worrying about him; he chose to go. And we've got to rescue the sheep. Come on.

[*They go out.*]

RENDALL [*as they go*]: How are we ever going to manage now – just the two of us?

[*Pause, during which the lights flicker uneasily and the knocking is heard again, first on one side then on the other.*]

AUNTIE [*putting her head out from the curtained alcove*]: Who's that knocking? Who's that knocking? Who's that knocking then?

[*The knocking is repeated while she comes out and stands mid-stage, vaguely looking about.*]

All right, I can hear you! Where is everybody? Rendall! Jake! Lem! Carilan! Can't anybody answer the door? [*Peevishly*] Where have they all got to? Sedna!

[*Knocking.*]

Have I got to open the door myself then? Fine thing to leave me all by myself to answer the door. [*She goes slowly to the door, opens it and looks out.*] Well, I never! There's nobody there! [*She returns to the fire to warm her hands, leaving the door open. Then she looks back.*] Have they all gone off and *left* me then? Rendall! Jake! Lem! Carilan! Sedna! Where *are* you? [*Pause; she starts to whimper.*] I'm not staying here all by myself! I'm not! I'm going to go after them! [*She goes quickly back to the alcove, gets coat, hat, moth-eaten old fox fur, scarf, stick, etc.*] I suppose they thought they'd all go shopping and leave me behind! Yes, that's what it is. They've gone shopping and didn't want to take me. Selfish lot! I'm not going to be left; I want to go around the shops, too. Wonder if they've got a Woolworth's? Or a Marks and Spencer? Or a Boots, there's several things I'd like to get at Boots ... Here! Jakin, Jakin! Wait for me! [*She hurries out.*]

[*Knocking is heard again; the lights flicker, grow dimmer; finnaly go out.* CURTAIN.]

SCENE 4

Same scene as previous; it is now lit by candles and also by the flickering light of a bonfire somewhere outside the window; noise of wind, and a shrill whistling. RENDALL *is sitting staring at the fire. The door opens, and* LEM *comes in, snow-covered.*

LEM: I don't see how he can have got across; the storm's so bad now. But at least the bonfire should guide him if he tries to turn back. Calling or whistling's no good – the wind drowns it. I've piled plenty of driftwood on the fire; it might burn till daylight.

RENDALL: You don't think we should go out and look for him?

LEM: No, I don't! We'd lose each other in the blizzard, and then who would there be to look after Auntie?

RENDALL: How she can sleep in this gale!

LEM: Force twelve, I should think. [*He sings.*]

Force three makes ripples on the ocean;
Leaves and small twigs are in constant motion:
  We measure the gale
  By the Beaufort Scale,
  But heigh-ho,
  So fast they blow
No one can catch the flakes of snow . . .

Force five: canoes return to port as
Wavelets appear in inland waters;
  We measure the gale
  By the Beaufort Scale,
  But heigh-ho,
  So fast they blow
No one can catch the flakes of snow . . .

At seven the windward walker tires
And whistling is heard in telegraph wires
  We measure the gale
  By the Beaufort Scale,
  But heigh-ho,
  So fast they blow
No one can catch the flakes of snow . . .

Force nine: a wind of fifty knots
Dislodges slates and chimney pots;
  We measure the gale
  By the Beaufort Scale,
  But heigh-ho,
  So fast they blow
No one can catch the flakes of snow . . .

While untold havoc sweeps in the train
Of Wind Force Twelve, a Hurricane:
  We measure the gale
  By the Beaufort Scale,
  But heigh-ho,
  So fast they blow
No one can catch the flakes of snow . . .

[*The song could be omitted.*]

RENDALL: Do you think we ought to wake Auntie and give her some breakfast? I suppose it *is* breakfast-time – though it's still pitch-dark [*looks out of window*].

LEM: She'll have to get up sometime.

RENDALL [*going to* AUNTIE'*s alcove*]: She'll simply hate it if it's going to be dark all day – Lem! She's not there! Her bed's empty!

LEM: She must have gone out. Her coat's gone. And her stick. We'll have to go out and look for her.

RENDALL: But she must have been gone for *hours*! Since we were out after the sheep.

[*She is flinging on a coat when the door opens and* AUNTIE *totters in, snow-covered, white-faced, obviously in the last stages of exhaustion and looking years older.*]

Auntie! Where *have* you been?

[RENDALL *and* LEM *rush to her, lead her to the armchair; she collapses into it as soon as her coat is removed.*]

RENDALL: I'll make some herb tea. [*Puts kettle on.*] You keep rubbing her hands and feet, wrap a blanket round her.

AUNTIE [*moaning*]: So tired ... so tired ...

LEM [*rubbing her hands*]: Auntie dear, where *ever* did you go?

AUNTIE: Went after you ... all went shopping ... left me behind ...

[LEM *and* RENDALL *stare at one another.*]

RENDALL: We didn't go shopping, Auntie. We were out after a cragfast sheep. But where have *you* been? You never went across the ice?

AUNTIE: Over the ice ... but it was so cold ... so slippery ... Oh! I thought my poor heart would give out ... Jakin ... didn't hear me call ... then the wolf got him ...

LEM *and* RENDALL [*together*]: *Wolf got him?*

AUNTIE: Perhaps it was just a great grey cloud ... When it had gone ... no Jakin! Oh, I was frightened! ... Slipped down on the ice ... couldn't go on ...

[LEM *and* RENDALL *look at one another again.*]

RENDALL: But then – how ever in the world – *did* you get back, Auntie?

AUNTIE: Seemed as if – as if somebody took my arm, I suppose . . . helped me . . . [*Her head nods forward; she is either fainting or asleep.*]

[RENDALL *has made a cup of herb tea;* LEM *holds up* AUNTIE'*s head while* RENDALL *puts the cup to her lips. While they are doing so, the door opens, and* MRS MACROY *enters silently, dressed as in Act One with black shawl over her head.*]

RENDALL: I think she took a little then. Do you think we should let her rest now? [*Turning, she sees* MRS MACROY *and gasps.*] *Oh,* Mrs MacRoy! What a fright you gave me! I didn't know you were there. [*Pauses*] Perhaps – was it *you* who kindly helped our aunt back across the ice?

MRS MACROY: Aye, I helped her. Your fire guided us. But she should not have been out in such weather.

RENDALL: She must have gone while we were after a sheep . . . We're very grateful to you. Won't – won't you sit down and have some herb tea?

MRS MACROY: No. I'll not eat or drink. That is not why I came.

RENDALL: Oh, *goodness* – Have you come for your money? It's just that –

MRS MACROY: No, it is not for the money. That debt has been paid many times over, in kindness and comfort and love. Can ye not guess what brings me here?

RENDALL: No.

[MRS MACROY, *who has hitherto stood with her face covered by a shawl, now turns away from audience and unveils to* RENDALL *and* LEM, *revealing under the shawl* SEDNA'*s black-and-white skirt and a sweater like the one* RENDALL *made and* SEDNA'*s long dark hair; they gasp and shade their eyes.*]

MRS MACROY: Now do ye not recognize me?

LEM: Sedna! You *are* Sedna?

RENDALL [*doubtfully*]: *Our* little Sedna?

AUNTIE [*who has become increasingly restless, whimpering*]: Sedna! Where did *she* go to? Where's my baby?

[MRS MACROY *re-veils.*]

RENDALL: Oh, please leave your face uncovered – you are so beautiful.

MRS MACROY: It would harm you, child. No human can gaze for more than a moment on the uncovered face of Winter.

AUNTIE [*dreamily*]: There were four of them: Whitworth, fourteen, Pankhurst Lane; Shonfield, ninety-two, Laura Place; and the two from D'Arcy House. Bless their hearts, the little angels, sleeping so peacefully in their prams. [*Her voice dies away.*]

MRS MACROY: Hush! Hush now! There will be no more bairns for you to find and cherish. Go to sleep my friend.

[*She crosses to* AUNTIE *and lays hand on forehead,* AUNTIE *becomes still.*]

RENDALL [*in a low voice*]: Lem! Do you suppose those were our parents' names she suddenly remembered?

LEM [*nods*]: Yes, I think so. [*He comes to stand by* AUNTIE, *putting a hand on her shoulder.*]

RENDALL [*to* MRS MACROY]: Then – shan't we ever see our little Sedna any more? Won't she come back to us?

MRS MACROY: Who can say what you will see in the time that is to come?

LEM: Jake and Carilan – what has happened to them?

[MRS MACROY *makes a single sweeping-away gesture.*]

RENDALL [*piteously*]: But why? Why? What had they done that was so bad?

MRS MACROY: It was their own nature that led them to destruction. My servants, the elements, did no more than carry out their appointed tasks.

LEM: Your servants?

[*Pause while they listen; the wind rises to a supernatural howl outside.*]

MRS MACROY [*going to the window and calling out*]: Quiet, let you, with your howling!

[*The wind dies down.*]

RENDALL [*apprehensively glancing towards the window*]: What – what is going to happen to *us*?

MRS MACROY: So long as you remain under this kindly roof, nothing can harm you. As you protected the stranger, so will you be protected. Do not be frightened of them roaring out yonder.

LEM: I'm not frightened ...

RENDALL: I am! It's so wild and so dark – so terribly cold ...

MRS MACROY: Winter is nothing to fear, child! There will be splendours in winter that summer can never equal. In winter the whole power and pride of nature is unloosed. Cold? Aye, but cold is the essence of truth. Dark? It is in darkness that all thought is born, that all living things germinate and begin to grow. Darkness will be the source of all discoveries, all visions. So let you not fear the dark.

RENDALL [*taking a deep breath*]: I'll try not to. But shall we have to stay here always?

MRS MACROY: No, child, only till the spring. When the sun first climbs over the southern ice, then, before the thaw comes, you may walk away from Winter Island. Until then, wait, listen, watch and learn.

RENDALL: But what about Auntie? If we go, what's going to happen to her?

MRS MACROY: Do not be anxious for her; she is in my keeping. She has no other need.

LEM: If we are not to go outside, what will happen to our animals?

MRS MACROY: I have laid my hand upon them; they will sleep until it is spring. Now I must be about my work; I will say farewell to you, for the time. Watch well –

[*The stage becomes dark, and* MRS MACROY *goes out; beyond the window, a display of Northern Lights can be seen, growing;* LEM *and* RENDALL *are seen silhouetted on either side of* AUNTIE; *they gaze out; she remains motionless.*]

LEM: There, you see. It's beautiful! I'm sure you've no need to be frightened.

RENDALL: Just the same, I am a bit frightened. Do you think you could sing something, Lem? Just – just till I get used to it?

LEM [*sings*]:

Hushabye, baby,
Dream a fine dream;
Ice will be forming
Over the stream;

Hibernate, baby,
Listen and learn;
Sooner or later,
Spring will return.

[CURTAIN.]

WINTERTHING

Songs

WORDS BY JOAN AIKEN
MUSIC BY JOHN SEBASTIAN BROWN

Tinker, Tailor

This song is from page 28

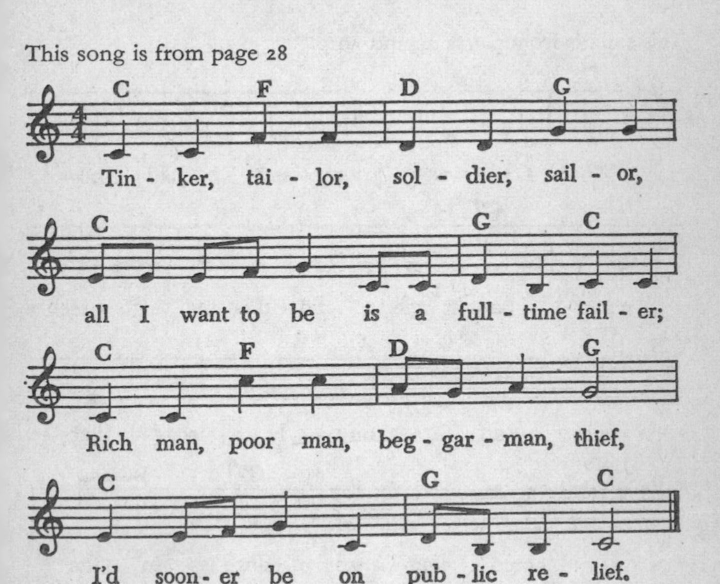

Army, navy, medicine, law,
Seems that in my nature there's a fatal flaw;
Doctor, lawyer, commander-in-chief,
What's the good of trying, I'd only come to grief.

This year, next year, sometime, never,
Failure crowns my best endeavour;
Science, art, or literature,
What's the good of doing it? It's all been done before.

When I Was Young

This song is from pages 29 and 30

When I was young and out for kicks,
I brought me a violin for one-and-six,
But the only song that I could remember
Was dance in July and sleep in December.

When I was young, in a reckless manner,
I bought me a fiddle for one-and-a-tanner,
But the only tune that box could play
Was bed in December and breakfast in May.

HUSHABYE

This song is from pages 33–4 and 61

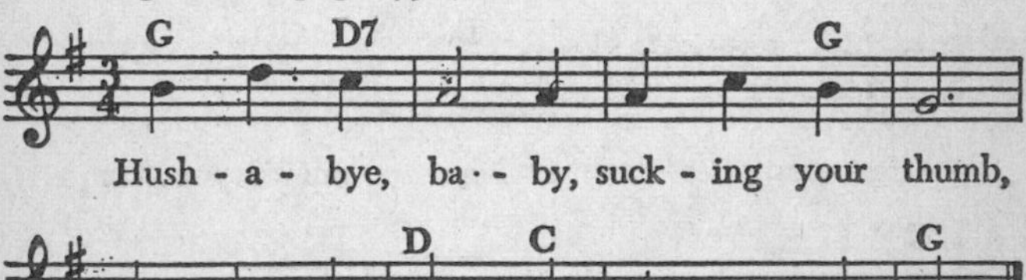

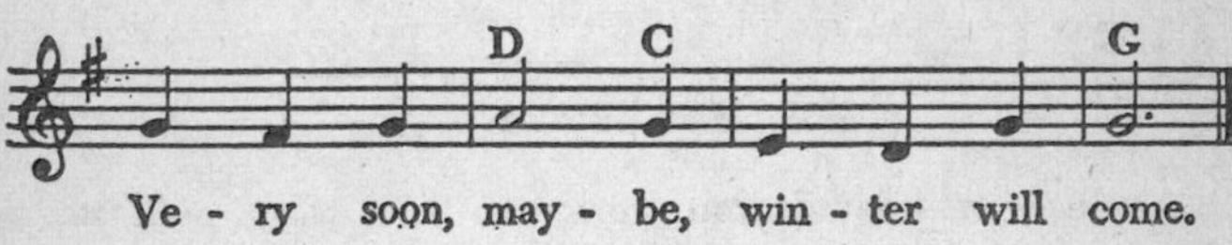

Hush, little Sedna,
Hear the wind blow;
Dream of the island
Covered in snow.

Hushabye, baby,
Dream a fine dream;
Ice will be forming
Over the stream;

Fish will be sleeping
Under the ice.
Hushabye, baby,
That's my advice.

Hibernate, baby,
Slumber and learn;
Sooner or later
Spring will return.

(*Repeat verse three.*)

Hibernate, baby,
Listen and learn;
Sooner or later,
Spring will return.

REMEMBER

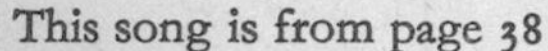
This song is from page 38

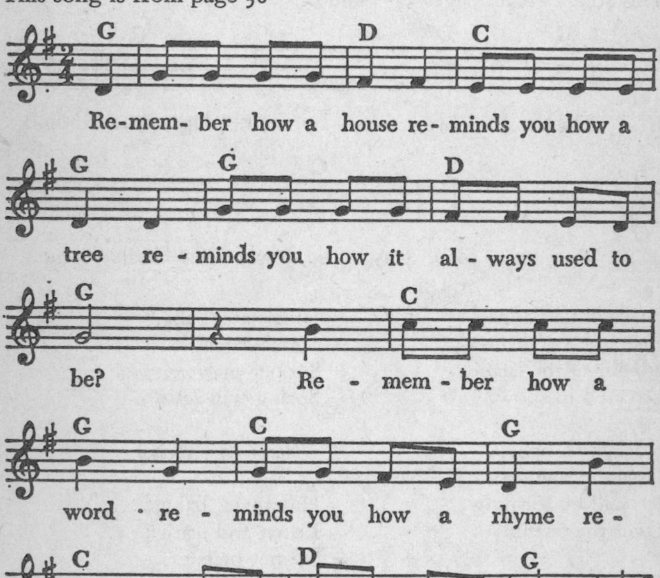

Remember how a smile
Reminds you how a face
Reminds you of some distant
Other place?

Remember how the sun
Reminds you how the snow
Reminds you how it all was
Long ago?

Dark

This song is from pages 40 and 43

(*Note: the chords in parentheses may be played with a capo on the 7th fret.*)

If dark cost money,
Rich people only
Would be able to pay
And rest them from day.

If dark were not given
Each night from heaven,
On field and town and park
Men would have to make dark.

Dark is so warm, so deep.
Without dark, how could we sleep?

(*Repeat first and last verses.*)

WINTER

This song is from page 51

Your hands will freeze, your nose, your knees,
Your fingers all turn blue.
Just rub them with a pinch of snow,
There's nothing else to do
– And I daresay we'll get through.
– And I daresay we'll get through.

The Beaufort Scale

This song is from page 56

Force five: canoes return to port as
Wavelets appear in inland waters;
We measure the gale
By the Beaufort Scale,
But heigh-ho,
So fast they blow
No one can catch the flakes of snow ...

Winterthing

At seven the windward walker tires
And whistling is heard in telegraph wires
We measure the gale
By the Beaufort Scale,
But heigh-ho,
So fast they blow
No one can catch the flakes of snow . . .

Force nine: a wind of fifty knots
Dislodges slates and chimney pots;
We measure the gale
By the Beaufort Scale,
But heigh-ho,
So fast they blow
No one can catch the flakes of snow . . .

While untold havoc sweeps in the train
Of Wind Force Twelve, a Hurricane:
We measure the gale
By the Beaufort Scale,
But heigh-ho,
So fast they blow
No one can catch the flakes of snow . . .

THE MOONCUSSER'S DAUGHTER

This play was first presented at the Arts Theatre, London, by the Unicorn Theatre for Young People on 7 April 1973. The cast was as follows:

Saul Bilkanchor	*Sion Probert*
Ruth	*Matyelok Gibbs*
Fred	*Gary Fairhall*
Sympathy	*Jacqueline Andrews*
Lord Boss	*Eric Leroy*
Fever	*Richard Jason*
Gritty	*Ian Ruskin*
Sunup	*Terry O'Sullivan*
Macawmack	*Marina McConnell*
Waitress	*Marina McConnell*

Directed by Ursula Jones
Designed by Pamela Howard

A NOTE BY THE DIRECTOR

The Mooncusser's Daughter is one of those rare plays for children that shows a respect for both its audience and its actors. As in all her work, Joan Aiken gives her audience full range for their imaginative abilities, and her actors a stimulating task that draws fully on their creativity. Although first performed by adult actors there is little in the play that a child actor might find too difficult to cope with.

SETTING THE PLAY

This can be done in numerous ways. At its simplest one could dispense with everything but the lift doors and the bottle from which *Caliban* emerges and rely on lighting or just action to move the play from one area to another.

The Unicorn Company performed the play on a small proscenium stage so lack of space caused us to use a more complex setting. The lighthouse was built of scaffolding on three levels; the top and smallest level being a gallery and lamp room; the central level was the living room (where half the action of the play takes place) and the lowest (stage level) was the cave. During the First Act the cave was concealed by a textured wall and steps curving round the lowest level – the steps serving as an entrance into the lighthouse. This left the rest of the stage clear for hotel and cliff top scenes. During the Second Act the wall and steps slid back, the bottle and rocky ledge came in and the whole of the stage was then used for the cave.

REHEARSING THE PLAY

This was always rewarding, but problems did crop up which are discussed later.

From its opening the play is wrapped round by the sea – its changes, its effect on the light and weather, its effect on everybody's lives since it is part of *Caliban*'s prison. It is everywhere, even in the glamour of the *Boss*'s hotel terrace. We found the resulting physical contrasts in each of the scenes to be an integral part of that scene.

The play is extremely funny and at times terrifying. For example, young audiences are, to say the least, unnerved after *Caliban*'s break out and tremendously relieved by *Sunup*'s line 'Blimey, what a smell of fish'. Throughout the play appalling or moving moments are both eased and interrupted by such lines as this, but curiously the company found this quite difficult to master.

It also has quite a complicated plot, drawing as it does on *The Tempest* and *The Winter's Tale*. So our chief concern was to bring out the clarity of the story line. To do this we had to ensure, for instance, that the extravagant *Boss,* with his almost revue-like scenes, should still remain so real that he and his henchmen seemed a true menace both to *Sympathy* as an individual and to the world in general. *Boss*'s performance, and the degree of his threat, relies heavily on his three employees. While he plays at bouncing on globes and flying kites, their nervousness of him and his huge power makes it clear that he is totally ruthless and will stop at nothing to gain his ambition. Of the henchmen, *Gritty* undergoes the greatest development.

We found it useful to look at the actions of the group and what they actually do. We noticed that unlike *Boss*, *Fever*, and *Sunup*, *Gritty*, though he lies, invents and deceives, never performs an act of violence. This and his constant singing (which was built up during rehearsal to irritate his companions) made him a different type of criminal – and it followed that his 'I feel bad about the girl' and his attempt to rescue *Sympathy* was an interesting swerve in direction rather than a sudden change of heart.

Saul with his histrionic remorse, jealousy guarding his guilt till (like Leontes) he practically destroys his wife and child, is isolating himself both physically and spiritually until he becomes the lonely creature wailing that he has relinquished everything in him that can bring understanding or comfort. As with *Boss*, we found we must begin with an odd but real man – a man whose violence frequently makes a fool of him, he trips on his socks, falls into cages and becomes increasingly exasperated by his wife's refusal to respond to his wailing with anything but calm and affection. Once *Saul*, despite his oddness, was 'real', the merge with *Caliban* was as shocking and disturbing as we felt the author intended. It seemed to double his violence and bring it under an alarming control that made the outcome of his final clash with *Sympathy* much more 'touch and go'. This rounding out of *Saul* was largely achieved by an improvisation between *Ruth* and *Sympathy* during rehearsals. I mention this stress on plausibility because we found the play deceptive. Its clear moods led us into thinking we'd achieved more than we had. Although we quickly agreed on issues such as the book (Prospero's in our production) and worked out the complexities of the *Saul/Caliban* merger to our satisfaction, we were skating still over the top of the play which had much more information to give us. Not until we had really explored, for example: *Sunup*'s criminal innocence or amorality; *Sympathy*'s innocence, corrupted by her own good intentions; the *Macaw-mack*'s animal innocence, programmed to a pattern of comic and pedestrian truths, could we eliminate an over-simplification that had crept in. That gone, we were able to use all the lightness and irony of the text, which pervades even the most electrifying scenes, and to relish as much as the audience the justice and rewards implacably meted out to all the characters.

URSULA JONES

CHARACTERS

SAUL BILKANCHOR, lighthouse-keeper of Sabretooth Light
RUTH, his wife
FRED, Saul's brother, a ghost
SYMPATHY, Saul's daughter, aged about nineteen
LORD BOSS, a king of crime
FEVER, GRITTY, SUNUP — employees of Lord Boss
MACAWMACK, a bird
CALIBAN
WAITER

The action of the play takes place on the sea-coast of Bohemia.

ACT ONE

Prelude
Scene 1: The lighthouse living-room
Scene 2: A hotel on Sabretooth Cliff
Scene 3: Lighthouse lamp-room
Scene 4: The cliff-top
Scene 5: The hotel
Scene 6: The lighthouse living-room
Scene 7: The cliff-top
Scene 8: Another part of the cliff-top
Scene 9: The lighthouse living-room
Scene 10: The lighthouse living-room
Scene 11: The lighthouse lamp-room
Scene 12: The lighthouse living-room

ACT TWO

Scene 1: The cave
Scene 2: The lighthouse living-room
Scene 3: The cave
Scene 4: The lighthouse living-room
Seene 5: The cave
Scene 6: The lighthouse living-room

Mooncusser was a word, used on the New England coast, for a wrecker.

Note: The music for all the songs in this play appears on pp. 134–44. It gives basic rhythms amd melodies for the songs, which the composer suggests the performers may vary if they wish.

ACT ONE

PRELUDE

Sabretooth Lighthouse is first seen far off, illuminated; then silhouetted. Then complete dark. Ray of light as from revolving lighthouse lantern travels over stage and audience. Darkness.

MAN'S VOICE [*singing*]:

Then three times around went our gallant ship,
Then three times around went she;
Then three times around went our gallant ship
And she sank to the bottom of the sea, the sea, the sea,
And she sank to the bottom of the sea . . .

[*Speaking slowly*] Then three times.

WOMAN'S VOICE: Three times, thrice, one two three; three repetitions, first time, second time, third time –

MAN'S VOICE: Then three times around went our gallant . . .

WOMAN'S VOICE: Gallant, handsome, fine, brave, valiant, heart of oak . . .

MAN'S VOICE: Ship . . .

WOMAN'S VOICE: Boat, vessel, bark, brig, schooner, liner, submarine –

MAN'S VOICE: For heaven's sake – we're thirty seconds over time as it is.

WOMAN'S VOICE: Cut out the last verse then –

MAN'S VOICE: And she sank to the bottom of the sea . . .

WOMAN'S VOICE: The sea, the ocean, the main, the deep, waves, tides, salt water.

MAN'S VOICE: And she sank to the bottom of the sea, the sea, the sea.
And she sank to the bottom of the sea.

WOMAN'S VOICE: That ends our programme of English by

radio for seafarers. We'll be back tomorrow at the same time. Now, because we left out the last verse, you'll have to wait two minutes for the next item, news and weather. Goodbye till tomorrow.

[*Silence.*]

DIFFERENT MAN'S VOICE: Hullo, hullo, hullo, Caliban, are you there, Caliban, calling Caliban, can you answer me, Caliban? Calling Caliban, calling Caliban, over.

CALIBAN'S VOICE: Help, help, help, this is Caliban, this is Caliban, can you hear me? Who are you?

DIFFERENT MAN'S VOICE: Where are you, Caliban, where are you, can you give me your position? We want to help you, we're trying to help you.

CALIBAN'S VOICE: I'm in a box, in a ship, in a bottle, it's deep and dark and very cold, I'm shut in a box, it's dark, it's dark.

DIFFERENT MAN'S VOICE: Yes, but where is this box, Caliban, where is it? Quick, we haven't much time, can you give me your position, where are you, Caliban? Over.

CALIBAN'S VOICE: Below the cliff, under the whirlpool. Let me out, help me, help me, help me.

DIFFERENT MAN'S VOICE: What cliff, what cliff, can you tell me, Caliban? We want to help we, want to get you out.

CALIBAN'S VOICE: Sabretooth Light – the cliff by Sabretooth Light.

DIFFERENT MAN'S VOICE: What coast? What coast, Caliban?

CALIBAN'S VOICE: Bohemia. The sea-coast of Bohemia.

DIFFERENT MAN'S VOICE: How deep do you lie?

CALIBAN'S VOICE [*fading*]: Full fathom five . . .

DIFFERENT MAN'S VOICE: Hold on, Caliban, we'll be coming down for you – can't say when but it will be very soon – just you hold on – wait for us . . .

[MAN'S *voice fades and Big Ben strikes.*]

SCENE 1

Light increases on one side of stage to show interior of Sabretooth Lighthouse ground floor. Section of curved wall, door at side, window, pair of lift doors at rear. Stairs to upper gallery with door and suggestions of more stairs going on up. Rocking-chair, armchair, small table, cooking-stove, gunrack, cradle. Cobwebs everywhere. Sound of sea, gulls, throughout. RUTH BILKANCHOR, *who is blind and wears dark glasses, sits knitting and rocking in rocking-chair. She is thin, gentle, in her fifties, white hair plainly arranged, perhaps in a bun.* FRED'S GHOST, *dressed as a sailor but all in white, and with a white face, is sitting on the windowsill. He has a white yo-yo with which he plays a lot of the time.*

Lift music (a special tune which is played each time the lift is in motion) is played, lift doors open to admit SAUL BILKANCHOR, *who carries a large bucket.* SAUL *is about the same age as* RUTH, *with long white hair, whiskers and beard. Doors shut again.*

SAUL [*dumping down bucket*]: He's restless. Off his feed.

RUTH: Why is that?

SAUL: Maybe because the whirlpool is moving off a bit, down channel. He thinks he might get away – make a break for it. But he's wrong.

RUTH: Saul – why don't you let him go? I'm sure it can't be right to keep him shut up down there.

SAUL [*violently*]: Are you mad? Let him go? Never!

RUTH: It must be so boring for him down there in that bottle.

SAUL: No one's going to profit from my crime. Not me – not *anybody*.

RUTH: But . . .

SAUL [*pacing about*]: I'm accursed! I'm the outcast of mankind. [*He has taken off seaboots and is in socks with large holes; every now and then he trips.*] I'm a haunted man, I tell you.

RUTH [*knitting away*]: Yes, you do tell me. Often.

SAUL: I'm damned. I'm doomed.

RUTH: Yes, dear.

SAUL: For twenty years a curse has lain on me.

RUTH: Nineteen this March.

SAUL: I'm a reject, I'm a throw-out, I live in exile.

RUTH: That's right.

SAUL: Oh, why did I follow the dreadful trade, why did I do it?

RUTH: Well, dear, for ten years you used to say you did it for kicks. Then, for the last nine, you've been saying you did it because Society owed you more than a lighthouse-keeper's salary of four pounds a year with free fishing and electricity.

SAUL: Free electricity! Pah! I live in a darkness of my own making, haunted by the thought of a brother's unforgiving ghost.

RUTH [*patiently*]: Look, Saul, for the umpteenth time, Fred *has* forgiven you. He forgave you right after it happened, nineteen years ago. Didn't you, Fred?

FRED'S GHOST [*moving forward*]: That's right. Never one to bear a grudge, I wasn't. Anyhow – easy berth being a ghost. No worries. Go wherever you like. Except I mostly like to stay here. Better than all that running I used to have to do – bun-running, gum-running, rum-running, gun-running, mum-running – *I'm* certainly not complaining. No more running for old Fred.

RUTH: See? He's forgiven you. He says so.

SAUL [*who can't see or hear* FRED]: Haunted, haunted, I tell you, by my past crimes – [*tripped by his flapping sock, he falls heavily.*] Oh, flaming Hades, Ruth, I wish you'd mend my socks.

RUTH [*calmly*]: Dear, I've told you over and over that mending socks is a thing you just can't do when you're blind. I'm knitting you this new pair, they'll be finished by tomorrow . . .

SAUL [*taking no notice*]: But still, it's *right* that I should suffer. It's *right* that I should be wretched.

RUTH: Now if you'd allow little Sympathy to come home, I daresay *she'd* do a bit of mending for you.

SAUL: Never!

RUTH: Helpful little thing she used to be.

SAUL: My daughter must never return to this accursed spot.

RUTH [*sighing*]: Fancy not wishing for your own daughter.

SAUL: The dead ground where a crime was committed is no place to bring up a child. Besides, I never did care for brats: always asking questions, wanting piggybacks – or ice-cream – losing their balls over the cliff –

RUTH: Anyway, Sympathy's turned nineteen, you could hardly call her a child now. Suppose she's homesick?

SAUL [*pacing about so energetically that* FRED *has a difficult job keeping out of his way*]: I tell you she shall not re-enter these tainted walls.

RUTH: Fred, do come and sit by the fire. It makes me nervous when Saul gets like this, I keep thinking he'll tread on you. And you might give little Jennet a bit of a rock; she's wakeful, the angel.

[FRED *obediently squats and rocks cradle.*]

SAUL: Isn't it nearly dinner-time? I'm devilish hungry.

RUTH: I'll just finish turning this heel, then I'll put on the milk.

SAUL: Bread-and-milk *again*? Can't we have a change from everlasting bread-and milk?

RUTH [*apologetically*]: They're the only things that get delivered. Now I can't go shopping bread-and-milk's all I can manage –

SAUL [*sourly*]: In that case don't trouble. I'll finish what Caliban left. [*He eats out of bucket with spoon.*]

[*Door opens, a voice shouts* Postman! *and a letter is tossed through.*]

RUTH [*joyfully*]: Oh, it'll be a letter from Sympathy!

SAUL: How do you know?

RUTH: Nobody else writes to us. Do read it aloud, there's a love.

SAUL: Why should I. She doesn't write to *me*.

RUTH [*patiently*]: Look, dear, you keep forgetting that for the last five years I've been blind. I'd ask Fred but we've tried before; he can't. Go on – do – you know you'll like to hear her news. I wonder if she's passed her exams.

SAUL [*exasperated*]: Oh – my life is just one long penance. But that's right. That's as it should be. [*Picks up letter, rips it open.*] 'Dear Mum. I hope you are well. Why do you never write to me any more?'

RUTH [*sighing*]: Eh, dear – What else does she say?

SAUL: 'I have finished at ballet school and got my diploma and I'm fed up with being away from home, so I'm coming back for a bit and shall arrive on Tuesday . . .'

RUTH: Tuesday! But that's *today*! Oh I am pleased!

SAUL [*still reading*]: 'Tell Dad' – *well*, of all the unnatural, spiteful little – I was quite right to send her away –

RUTH: Why? What does she say?

SAUL: 'Tell Dad if he doesn't want to see me he can sit up in the lamp room or go down in the cave or jump off the cliff, I don't care which. Lots of love dearest Mum from Sympathy.' Well, that settles it. She's not coming here. If I see her coming it's her own responsibility – I shall warn her off just as I would anybody else. [*He takes gun – a large bell-mouthed blunderbuss – from rack and goes upstairs.*]

RUTH: Oh dear. Has he taken the gun, Fred?

FRED'S GHOST: Yes.

RUTH: That's going to be awkward. What shall we do?

FRED: I dunno.

SCENE 2

Light shifts to other side of stage. Hotel balcony on edge of cliff. Signs of luxury: plants in gold pots, champagne in bucket. LORD BOSS *is sitting in elaborate deck-chair shooting sucker-darts at large target. He is a very poor shot. Dressed in tropical beachwear.*

LORD BOSS: Waiter!

[*Waiter rushes in.*]

WAITER: My lord?

BOSS: What have you got on the lunch menu?
WAITER: Everything – everything, my lord.
BOSS: I don't believe you. What haven't you got?
WAITER: My lord?
BOSS: Come on, come on – Have you got shark's fin?
WAITER: Yes, my lord.
BOSS: Long pig?
WAITER: F–f–fairly long.
BOSS: Larks' tongues?
WAITER [*doubtfully*]: There's lark *pie*; I daresay we could take the tongues out and serve them separately –
BOSS: Bird's-nest soup?

[WAITER *is silent.*]

Well, speak up, man – have you got it or haven't you?
WAITER [*desperately*]: We could have some flown over from China – I'm afraid lunch might be a little late –
BOSS [*dangerously*]: Well, just you *get* some flown over. And lunch had better *not* be late or it's unlikely I shall stay at this hotel again – it's unlikely *any*one will ever stay at this hotel again –
WAITER: Y–y–yes, my lord ... [*He starts out, running, then runs back to say*] The three gentlemen you wanted are here to see you, my lord – Mr Fever, Mr Gritty and Mr Sunup –
BOSS: About time, too. Well, don't stand there looking like last year's calendar, send them in. And get that bird's-nest by one o'clock –

[WAITER *shows in* FEVER, GRITTY *and* SUNUP, *then dashes off.* FEVER *and* SUNUP *are tough-looking, middle-aged gangsters; very short haircuts; stubble on chins.* GRITTY *is the youngest of the three, about twenty, with long, curly hair and glasses; he has an absent-minded expression and may carry a guitar.*]

BOSS: Well? Did you find out where the book is? Fever?
FEVER: Yes, boss.

[SUNUP *nudges him.*]

Er – yes, my lord.
BOSS: Where is it?
FEVER: It's like you thought. It's still in the wreck of the

Miranda, which is lodged in the cave at the foot of Sabre-tooth cliff.

BOSS: Right. Send along a dredger this afternoon and haul the whole wreck up to the top.

FEVER: Can't do that, my lord.

BOSS [*not pleased*]: Oh? Why not?

FEVER: There's a whirlpool every high tide. Caliban's Cauldron, the locals call it. Any ship gets close to those cliffs is a write-off. The dredger wouldn't stand a chance. They say even the sea-serpent got himself corkscrewed down into the whirlpool once and he's never been able to unwind himself since.

BOSS: Send down a diver, then.

FEVER: He'd get smashed up too.

BOSS: For the love of Mercury – do I have to go *myself*?

FEVER [*hastily*]: No, no, boss, listen, it's like this: well, see, the only way to get to the foot of the cliff is from the light-house – there's twenty miles of those cliffs, all as sheer as an office block. And the cave's right under the lighthouse – there's supposed to be a way down, a stair or a path or summat –

GRITTY: A lift, *I* heard –

BOSS: And so?

FEVER: Well, there's some crazy old character in the light-house who won't let anyone in. Says there's a curse on the place. Has a blunderbuss. Threatens to shoot anyone who sets foot.

BOSS: Well, shoot *him*.

FEVER: That won't wash either, my lord.

BOSS: Why, *why*?

FEVER: They say down in this cave there's a big rock, like, balanced on a kind of a spur. Right up above the ship. If this old guy was to do something, pull some lever –

GRITTY: Let off a firecracker, *I* heard –

FEVER: The rock falls and the ship's smashed to blazes.

BOSS: In which case *you'd* be smashed too. Of that you can be *quite* sure. Well, you'll just have to use cunning. Pretend you're the window-cleaner. Get into that lighthouse somehow. Then –

FEVER: Then that's not the only complication.

BOSS: A lot of *geniuses* I have working for me. All I want is to get hold of an old book out of a ship that's been lying under water for twenty years – anyone would think I was trying to get the gold out of Fort Knox. Well?

FEVER: The book has a guardian.

BOSS: A guardian? You mean there's someone down there in the wreck keeping an eye on it – I suppose you're going to tell me it's the sea-serpent?

FEVER: Something of the kind, my lord.

GRITTY: We managed to get in touch with it on VHF. It has a name – Caliban.

FEVER: Told us it had been left in charge of the book. By the previous owner.

BOSS: Oh, this is just great. Loonies in the lighthouse, werewolves in the wreck – going to tell me you're scared?

FEVER: No, but all these difficulties have put the price up. Five thousand we want now.

BOSS: Three. Not a penny more.

[*The three glance at one another, shake heads.*]

FEVER: Four. And that's our last word.

BOSS: You get four. I get the book by this time tomorrow. Otherwise I get me some other helpers. Okay?

[*They nod.*]

So, where were we?

GRITTY: We were telling you about Caliban.

BOSS: *What* about Caliban?

GRITTY: Caliban says he won't give up the book unless we fetch down somebody that's single in spirit.

BOSS: Single in *spirit*?

GRITTY: Those are the rules, he says. Someone free from the taint of deceit.

FEVER: In other words, some bloke what's never told a lie in all his life.

BOSS: Then you'll have to find someone, won't you?

FEVER: Have a heart, guvnor, how are we going to set about that?

BOSS: There's no reason why I should do your job for you, but as it happens I've got something that might help – [*He goes through balcony door.*]

GRITTY [*begins to wander about, singing to himself*]:

> Who is Caliban, who is he?
> Everyone seems to wonder;
> Sleeping down below the sea,
> Snoring away like thunder,
> Fifty-five fathoms under –

FEVER: What beats me is *why* the boss should want an old book that's been down at the bottom of the sea for nearly twenty years.

GRITTY [*singing*]:

> Eels he has where he oughta have hair,
> Hands and feet are suckers,
> Breathes in brine instead of air,
> Makes a horrible ruckus,
> Sounds like a boiler in bad repair –

– I daresay the boss wants that book because it's just about the only thing that he hasn't got already.

FEVER: Yes, but what does he want it *for*?

BOSS [*reappearing so suddenly that he makes them jump*]: That book's been at the bottom of the sea a lot longer than twenty years, Fever.

FEVER [*recovering*]: But, like I said, what'd you want it for, guvnor? You're the richest man in the world as it is.

BOSS: So there's no point in making myself richer, is there? I can't look at a different movie with each eye. Can't sail two yachts at once. Can't drink six glasses of champagne at the same time. [*He is holding a glass paperweight-type ball with a ship inside it, which he tosses to* FEVER.] Hold that, and count ten.

FEVER: One, two, three, etc.

BOSS [*simultaneously with* FEVER]: What would you do if you were the richest man in the world, Gritty?

GRITTY: Sit in the sun all day and make up tunes.

FEVER [*dropping the ball, which bounces*]: Stap me, the flaming thing's red hot, why didn't you say?

BOSS [*retrieving ball, tossing it to* GRITTY]: Hold it and count ten –

FEVER [*rubbing his burnt hand*]: If *I* was the richest bloke in the world I'd make a big bomb and blow up my old woman.

GRITTY: Four, five, six – you're not burning *my* fingers off . . . [*He drops the ball in the ice-bucket.*] How does it get that way?

BOSS; I've done everything I can with money. Now what I want is power –

GRITTY: To do what?

BOSS: Change the weather. Fill in the Mediterranean. Make a ski-resort in the Sahara. [*There is a large globe on the balcony; he inverts it, spins it, and sits on top.*] I want to turn the world upside down. Flatten the Himalayas. Melt the icecaps. Chop down all the forests. See? Now, you take that ball and find me somebody who's never told a lie.

FEVER [*puzzled*]: I don't quite get you, boss.

BOSS: Find me somebody who can hold that ball while they count ten –

SCENE 3

The lamp-room of the lighthouse. One huge light, surrounded by a glass chimney like an old-fashioned oil lamp. It is switched off. Window. SAUL *is polishing the chimney and looking from time to time out of the window, where he has his blunderbuss propped.* FRED *glides in and begins hypnotizing* SAUL *by means of arm-waving dance.* SAUL *doesn't see it but is insensibly influenced.*

FRED [*singing*]:

Full fathom five thy brother lies,
His buttons turned to haddock's eyes,
Nothing of him now is found
Save a ghost that floats around
Two feet off the ground,
Some might find this rather strange,
But not old Fred; he likes the change.

[SAUL *slowly falls asleep leaning farther and farther over the gun which finally goes off without waking him.*]

SCENE 4

Edge of cliff, indicated by one or two tufts of grass and distant view of lighthouse as in Prelude. SYMPATHY *comes in carrying duffel bag, followed by* GRITTY.

SYMPATHY: Well, thanks for the lift. Hope I didn't bring you out of your way.

GRITTY: No you haven't. As a matter of fact – I want to ask a favour of *you* now –

SYMPATHY: Sure. What is it?

GRITTY: You live in the lighthouse –

SYMPATHY: Well – I used to. But my dad said an awful crime had been committed there and it wasn't a proper place for a child. So he sent me off to boarding-school.

GRITTY: I've heard the locals say the lighthouse is haunted –

SYMPATHY: That's right. By my uncle Fred and my little cousin Jennet. Oh I *am* looking forward to seeing Jenny again. She was such a little duck – always laughing, never grizzled –

GRITTY: You've *seen* them? The ghosts?

SYMPATHY: Of course. I used to play with Jenny all the time when I was little –

GRITTY: Strewth. Excuse me, would you mind holding this a moment while I polish my glasses. [*He pulls glass ball wrapped in a handkerchief from his pocket, unwraps and hands it to* SYMPATHY, *polishes his glasses.*] But why do the ghosts of your uncle and cousin haunt the place?

SYMPATHY: Uncle Fred's ship got wrecked in the channel. Little Jenny was on board. They were both drowned. I suppose the lighthouse was the nearest bit of land for them to haunt on –

GRITTY: I see.

SYMPATHY: But what was the favour you wanted to ask? Not just for me to hold this? [*Playing toss and catch with ball.*] It's pretty. [*She examines it.*] Uncle Fred's ship is sunk in the big cave at the foot of the cliff. They say a great crystal stalactite has formed all round it so it's like a ship in a bottle –

GRITTY: Well I was wondering if you could help me. It's this way – I'm a student of Marine Psychology – doing a research project on dolphins' dreams –

SYMPATHY: Do dolphins have dreams?

GRITTY: Why not? You see ghosts. Dolphins have dreams. Thanks –

[*He puts on glasses, holds out hand for ball; she tosses it to him; he feels it in amazement, hurriedly wraps it in his handkerchief again and replaces it in his pocket.*]

There's a dolphin out in that channel, you see. I've got into communication with it on VHF, now I want to study it face to face –

SYMPATHY: It's not going to be easy. There's a whirlpool in the channel – if you aren't careful you'll be drowned for sure –

GRITTY: I know. That's why I wanted to get into your dad's lighthouse – I heard there was a way down to the cave, thought I might get a look at the dolphin from there.

SYMPATHY: Yes, Dad built a lift down so he could go and look at the wreck and feel miserable –

GRITTY: I went up there but he fired his gun at me through

the window. So I wondered if I could come along with you. Maybe you could say I was a friend of yours . . .?

SYMPATHY: But you aren't a friend of mine. We've only just met.

GRITTY [*taken aback*]: Well – but – we might *get* to be friends. I – I'd *like* to – I could pay you quite a bit, too, I've got this grant –

SYMPATHY: I'm afraid it wouldn't be possible, I don't even know if my father will let *me* in. And he'd *never* stand for my bringing in a boyfriend –

GRITTY [*swallowing*]: Maybe I could dress up as a girl? Say I was a school friend of yours?

SYMPATHY: But that would be telling a lie.

[*Deadlock.* GRITTY *looks at her blankly. She smiles goodbye and goes.* FEVER *and* SUNUP *rise up from behind grass tussocks where they have been concealed. They all look at each other and shrug.*]

GRITTY [*singing*]:

Let's leave Caliban, let him lie,
It's tough enough to be him,
No use dragging him high and dry,
Nobody wants to see him,
Bye bye, Caliban, bye bye bye . . .

FEVER [*uneasily*]: What d'you reckon Caliban *is*?

GRITTY: Some kind of monster? Maybe he is the sea-serpent.

FEVER: Why should he want someone who's never told a lie?

GRITTY: To eat? Maybe they're tenderer that way. Crazy bit of luck that girl's one of these no-lie marathon types –

FEVER [*sourly*]: Except that she wouldn't co-operate.

GRITTY [*airily*]: Oh, I'll soften her up presently, you'll see. Or else we could kidnap her. Bit of a shame, though, if the monster eats her, quite a pretty girl –

FEVER: All for a crummy old book.

GRITTY: Mind you, I've been chatting up the locals down in the port and there's legends about that crummy old book that would make a hardboiled egg grow whiskers –

FEVER: Such as?

GRITTY: It's got all the secrets that's ever been wrote. Like how to make human beings, and go faster than light, and spin rhubarb and string vests out of the sun's rays –

FEVER [*thoughtfully*]: Handy kind of thing to have about. Seems a bit of a waste to pass it over to old Boss; he's got all he needs –

GRITTY [*singing*]:

Who doth not want a thing
Except a place to sing
And a fire to warm his feet
In winter's wet and sleet,
Give over, give over, give over,
The book of all knowledge,
As good as a college,
Some know-how is better than fruitless endeavour.

[*During the song,* SUNUP *tiptoes out.*]

FEVER: Where did Sunup go?

GRITTY: Dunno – he was here just now. I wonder why Caliban doesn't use the book himself.

FEVER: Maybe he doesn't need anything either. Or maybe he can't read – Sunup's pretty dumb; bit of a dead weight. If it weren't for him, you and I could split that four thousand between us –

[GRITTY *looks at him, rather startled.*]

SCENE 5

Hotel. LORD BOSS *flying kite.* SUNUP *enters conspiratorially and follows him up and down as he plays string.*

SUNUP [*loud whisper*]: My lord! My lord! Hey, boss!

BOSS [*hearing him at last; annoyed*]: I didn't ask for you to come back. Well? What is it?

SUNUP: I thought as how you ought to know, boss, that that other precious pair . . .

BOSS: Fever and Gritty?

SUNUP: Fever and Gritty are planning to play the old pitch-and-toss on you. That book you're so keen to get your hooks on – they're fixing to keep it for themselves. Well, stands to reason, dunnit? Read the book, you got all the power in the world – they'd be suckers if they handed it over, wouldn't they?

BOSS [*coolly*]: Well? And why are *you* being so honest and telling me this? Wouldn't they cut you in?

SUNUP [*virtuously*]: *I* wouldn't do you, boss – my lord. Not after the long years I've worked for you. But I was thinking – if you'd like *me* to do the whole job – call them off, like –

BOSS: Then *you*'d get the whole four thousand, was that what you were thinking?

[SUNUP *nods, beaming.*]

And what's to stop *you* from doublecrossing me and keeping the book for yourself?

SUNUP: Why, what good would it be to me? I never learned to read, boss – anybody would tell you that –

[*The kite, an elaborate dragon/monster, suddenly flops out of the sky and lands on* SUNUP*'s head as he and* LORD BOSS *stare measuringly at one another.*]

SCENE 6

The lighthouse. RUTH *knitting.* FRED *wandering about with his yo-yo.*

RUTH: Animal, vegetable or mineral?

FRED: You know I'm no good at intellectual games.

RUTH: Please, Fred. It helps pass the time. I get so impatient, wondering when Sympathy will be here. Does the place look nice and welcoming?

FRED [*looking at cobwebs, shrugging*]: Yes. Fine. All right, animal.

RUTH: On land?

FRED: No.

RUTH: In the air?

FRED: No.

RUTH: In the sea?

FRED: Yes – I suppose so.

RUTH: Within five miles of here?

FRED: Yes.

RUTH: Is it Caliban?

FRED: See? You're too good at this game . . . Yes.

RUTH: Oh dear. Fred? Do you think Caliban really exists? Sometimes I wonder if Saul hasn't just invented him. As an excuse for going down to the cave –

FRED [*with certainty*]: Oh, no. No. Caliban exists all right. I've been down there. I've seen him.

RUTH: But why does Saul keep him shut up?

FRED: Dunno. Dunno which of them is really the jailer. Maybe Caliban keeps Saul shut up.

RUTH: What does he look like?

FRED: It's hard to say.

RUTH: D'you think he might ever get out and come up here?

[*They both look uneasily at the lift.*]

Fred! I can hear someone coming – it's Sympathy!

[RUTH *stands up, takes a few cautious steps towards the door.* SYMPATHY *opens it and rushes in.*]

SYMPATHY: Mum! Mum! [*Runs to* RUTH *and hugs her.*]

RUTH: Oh, dearie – I *am* pleased to see y— to have you back. [*Hugging her, running hands up arms, laying hand on top of head.*] You've grown so! My goodness, you must be nearly as tall as Dad –

SYMPATHY: Why are you wearing dark glasses, Mum?

RUTH: Oh – the light hurts my eyes a bit sometimes – it's nothing. But have you really finished at ballet school? Tell about your exams – did you do well?

SYMPATHY: Yes, got a first class.

RUTH: First class – that's wonderful! So now you're a real dancer –

SYMPATHY: That's right. Want to see?

[SYMPATHY *starts doing ballet steps.* RUTH *is looking in the wrong direction.*]

SYMPATHY: Mum! I'm over here.

[RUTH *obediently turns her head, but now* SYMPATHY *has moved again.*]

No, *here*, love –

[RUTH *turns, still in the wrong direction;* SYMPATHY *stands watching her, more and more puzzled.*]

RUTH: Where are you now, dearie?

SYMPATHY: I'm here, Mum.

[SYMPATHY *now slowly surveys the interior and takes in the cobwebs and general muddle; beginning to suspect the truth, she moves silently up behind* RUTH *and extends her hand from behind in front of* RUTH*'s face.* RUTH *doesn't see it.* SYMPATHY *then gently puts her hands on* RUTH*'s shoulders.* RUTH *starts violently.*]

RUTH: Oh – dearie – you startled me –

SYMPATHY [*deep anxiety*]: Mum? Can't you see *at all*?

RUTH: Well – no, darling – not really.

SYMPATHY: So *that's* why you haven't answered my letters for so long. How long have you been bl— like this?

RUTH: Oh – it took quite a while to come on – about five years.

SYMPATHY: But didn't you go to a doctor?

RUTH: You know how your father is about leaving this place –

SYMPATHY: Just wait till I see Father and give him a piece of my mind –

RUTH: Anyway, very likely a doctor wouldn't have been able to help. And I get on perfectly well.

SYMPATHY: Yes, but –

RUTH: I can knit socks for your father – and listen to the sea – you remember I always liked that best –

SYMPATHY: But –

RUTH: And I've got Fred and little Jenny for company –

SYMPATHY [*a little more cheerful*]: Oh well, I'm glad they're still here. Where are they?

RUTH: Why – right here – Fred was playing Twenty Questions with me just before you came, weren't you, Fred –

FRED: That's right. And she was beating me like she always does.

SYMPATHY [*puzzled*]: Fred's here? Where? I can't see him.

RUTH: And little Jennet's in her cradle, she doesn't grow a bit, the angel, not like you, darling –

SYMPATHY [*really distressed*]: But I can't see her *either*! [*Looking in cradle*] Oh, *nothing's* the way it should be.

RUTH [*sadly*]: I guess you've grown up, dearie – maybe that's why you can't see them any more. Your father never could, you know –

SYMPATHY: But you can –

RUTH: Yes, but I'm blind.

FRED [*warningly*]: Here's Saul coming –

[*The lift light has flashed green. Lift music. Doors open with a puff of green smoke.*]

SAUL [*emerging from lift with bucket*]: Something's definitely upsetting him – I don't like it.

[*He suddenley sees* SYMPATHY; *they stare at each other for a long, hostile pause.*]

Who are *you*?

RUTH: Saul! It's your own daughter.

SYMPATHY: As you perfectly well know.

SAUL [*putting down bucket, reaching for blunderbuss*]: Now look: I've said it before, I'm saying it again – I will not have you here. This is no place for –

SYMPATHY: No place for children. *I* know. You said it before and you got rid of me. But I'm not a child now – and I'm back and I'm staying. For as long as I choose. This is my *home* –

RUTH [*distressed*]: Oh, dearie! In a way he's right, you know – there won't be anything for you to do here. Your diploma for dancing will be just wasted.

SYMPATHY [*to* SAUL]: Why didn't you write and tell me she was going blind?

SAUL: What was the use?

SYMPATHY: Why didn't you take her to a doctor?

SAUL: I knew it. I knew if you came home you'd start making trouble –

SYMPATHY: You're just a selfish self-centred old *pig* –

SAUL: I've got plenty of worries of my own. I haven't time to attend to your –

SYMPATHY: Oh, I'm so angry I could *bash* you.

SAUL: Clear out!

SYMPATHY: Fancy letting your own wife go blind.

SAUL: Go away! Get out of here!

SYMPATHY: Not likely. *Look* at all this mess.

[*Ignoring* SAUL *and his blunderbuss she snatches up a long feather broom and starts whisking it about, narrowly missing* FRED, *who shrugs philosophically and keeps moving out of the way.*]

You're not getting rid of me again – *some*body's got to look after Mother –

RUTH: I don't really need looking after, you know, dearie.

SAUL [*more calmly, putting down gun, folding arms*]: You can't stay here. I need solitude.

SYMPATHY [*sweeping round his feet*]: Oh? And what do you need solitude *for*?

SAUL: To repent my crimes. This is a poisoned place.

SYMPATHY: Oh, that's right. I remember now. You used to go on like this before. So okay, what's it poisoned by?

SAUL [*cunningly*]: If I tell you, will you clear out? And leave me and your mother in peace?

SYMPATHY: If I go I'll take her with me.

RUTH: Oh, lovey, I couldn't live anywhere but here – I'm used to this place.

SAUL: All right, I'll tell you if that'll get rid of you. I was a Mooncusser.

[*From under a lot of cobwebs he drags out a large box which he has some difficulty in unlocking. He hoists up the stiff lid and takes out a number of miscellaneous objects, looks at them lovingly, and returns them to the box; they include a large painting, some mildewy bits of brocade, tarnished jewellery including a crown and sceptre, a microscope, bits of machinery of whose use he is obviously ignorant, a moulting fan, a helmet, archeological remains, etc.* SYMPATHY *watches, puzzled.*]

FRED [*singing, while* SAUL *opens the box*]:

When Force Twelve Gale doth loudly blow,
And whirlpools whirl and glow-worms glow,
And birds sit brooding in the snow,
And Gulf Stream reverseth towards Mexico,
And Mother Carey's chicks are hatched,
And mainsail do split and gotta be patched,
    Hey ding-a-ding
    We sing,
For all events but ours are scratched.

SYMPATHY: A Mooncusser? [*Pause.*] You mean a wrecker?

SAUL: I used to hang a bit of sacking over the lighthouse lamp. And then light a flare half a mile farther along the cliff, so ships would steer towards it and split themselves on Sabretooth Rock. [*Beating his breast.*] Many and many's the vessel that I've sent to the bottom in the old days.

SYMPATHY: And all this old junk's what you got off the ships?

SAUL: Things that used to get washed up on Sabretooth Rock.

SYMPATHY: What a collection of useless stuff.

SAUL: Oh, what an evil trade mine was! I shall never atone for it.

SYMPATHY [*thoughtfully*]: No, I don't see how you *can*. You must have finished off a lot of people who never did you any harm.

SAUL: Scores.

SYMPATHY: Why did you stop?

SAUL: It was after I married your mother.

SYMPATHY: Yes, I wouldn't think *she'd* stand for it.

RUTH: He didn't tell me about it. dearie – not till the end.
SAUL: It was sinking Fred's ship brought me up short.
FRED [*patiently*]: You *know* I don't hold it against you, Saulie –
SYMPATHY: *You* sank Fred's boat? Your own brother?
SAUL: My own brother.
SYMPATHY: On purpose?
SAUL [*irritably*]: No, no, of course not on purpose. He was a free-trader –
SYMPATHY: You mean a smuggler?
SAUL: The thing was, he didn't usually operate round here. Farther south was his run. How was I to know he'd be up this way? He was doing a special job for one of those professors at the university – fetching back art treasures from abroad.
SYMPATHY: But didn't you recognize his ship?
SAUL: It was at night, thick-head.
SYMPATHY: So what did you get from that haul?
SAUL: Oh, how can you ask such a heartless question?
SYMPATHY: I just wondered what there was on board.
SAUL: It was a lot of historical stuff dredged up from the bottom of the Mediterranean. Some other government was laying claim to it. The most important thing was a book the professor wanted.
SYMPATHY: What happed to the professor?
SAUL: He was on board. He was drowned too. They all were. My own brother! And his child. [*With a sudden access of guilt*] I killed them. Oh, what a wicked, wicked man I am.
SYMPATHY: Is it wickeder to kill your own brother than anyone else?
SAUL [*shocked*]: Your own family? Of course it is.
FRED: *Honest*, Saul, I know you didn't mean to do me in.
SYMPATHY [*indignantly*]: So just because you felt bad about killing Uncle Fred, you kept *me* away from my home all these years. Why should *I* be the one to suffer? What good did *that* do?

SCENE 7

The cliff-top. LORD BOSS *is bouncing about on a spacehopper painted like a globe, beside an elaborate tent.* SUNUP *comes in on tiptoe.*

SUNUP [*conspiratorially*]: Boss! Me lord!

BOSS [*looking at watch*]: Just a minute. Ten nine eight seven six five four three two one zero. [*He bounces as he counts.*]

[*Distant explosion.*]

SUNUP [*anxiously*]: What was that, Boss? You didn't blow up the lighthouse?

BOSS: No, the hotel. I told them they knew what to expect if the tea was cold once more. You'll have to find me another hotel.

SUNUP: There isn't any other hotel round here, my lord.

BOSS: Then you'll have to finish the job today. Why are you here, anyway? Have you got the book?

SUNUP: No.

BOSS [*irritably*]: Go and get on with the job, then.

SUNUP: But I soon will; look, I've found someone what's never told a lie. [*He pulls on the end of a long cord that he is holding, and a large red-and-blue bird waddles in.*]

BOSS [*unimpressed*]: *That?* What is it?

SUNUP [*proudly*]: It's a macaw. His name's Macawmack. He's never told a lie – have you, Mackie?

MACAWMACK: Keep off the grass. Give Way. Trespassers will be persecuted. Penalty Five Pounds. No smoking.

SUNUP: You see? He couldn't tell a lie if he tried. Could you, Mackie? But he cost a bomb, Boss; I'll need some more expenses.

BOSS [*not pleased*]: How much?

MACAWMACK: No litter. No parking. Don't lean out of the window. Dogs must not foul this footway.

SUNUP [*shouting in* MACAWMACK's *ear*]: Ssssh! [*To* BOSS] Three hundred.

[BOSS *reluctantly goes into tent.*]

SUNUP [*calling after him*]: And I'll need to borrow one of your condensed-air guns, me lord. Getting into the lighthouse is going to be tricky.

BOSS [*coming out with elaborate weapon and bundle of notes*]: Well, hurry up, will you? The weather's deteriorating. I'm not prepared to hang about here much longer.

[*Sky darkens, wind whistles, loud peal of thunder. The tent blows away.*]

SCENE 8

Another part of the cliff-top. FEVER *and* GRITTY *are huddling under large umbrella.*

FEVER: I don't think much of *your* plan. At this rate we're likely to be washed over the cliff before we ever get into the lighthouse.

GRITTY: For heaven's sake! Where's your subtlety? You've got to use subtlety with girls. I just laid a little posy with a photo of a dolphin on the lighthouse doorstep. That'll remind her of me.

FEVER [*disgustedly*]: A posy! Why should a dolphin remind her of you? You don't look like a dolphin.

GRITTY: Forget-me-nots and sea-lavender and dolphiniums.

FEVER: Did you see her?

GRITTY: No but she's bound to come out some time to take in the milk.

FEVER: How do you know they have milk delivered. I've never seen a milkman go up. Maybe they keep a goat.

GRITTY: Then she'll go out to milk the goat.

FEVER: In my opinion we'd better just blast our way in. I pinched one of the boss's condensed-air guns – thought it might come in handy –

GRITTY: Don't you see, you triple-distilled fool, if you do

that, then old Whiskers will pull the lever that topples over the rock that smashes the wreck, and we'll *never* get the flaming book? No, patience is the only answer.

[*sings*]

Tell me where is Patience mustered,
How can you stop from getting flustered,
How remain as cool as custard?
You must learn to meditate,
Don't be so precipitate,
Everything comes to chaps as wait,
Play it by ear, work to rule,
Whatever happens, keep your cool,
Keep your cool.

[SYMPATHY *comes running in.*]

SYMPATHY [*breathless*]: Oh, I'm so glad you're still here. I was afraid you might have left.

GRITTY [*triumphant glance at* FEVER]: There, what did I tell you? [*To* SYMPATHY]: Did you find my posy?

SYMPATHY: Posy, no, what posy?

[FEVER *returns* GRITTY'*s glance.*]

No, I came to ask you – to ask you to help me –

GRITTY: Anything we can do of course – oh, this is my mate –

SYMPATHY [*hasty nod to* FEVER]: Pleased to meet you. [*To* GRITTY] You did say – you said you had plenty of money –

GRITTY: Sure. At least we haven't actually got the cash on us, but we can get it from this chap who's giving us our grant –

FEVER: Grant, what grant?

[GRITTY *gives him warning kick.*]

SYMPATHY: You see my mother's gone blind – I want to get her to a doctor, but I've no money for the fee –

GRITTY [*easily*]: Yeah, we could help you with that. Take you and your mum into town on the bike, if you like.

SYMPATHY: Oh, that's kind of you – and I'll try to help you with your research.

FEVER: Research?

GRITTY: Yes, if we could just get a quick look at the dolphin first.

FEVER: Dolphin?

[GRITTY *scowls at him.*]

SYMPATHY: Yes, I've been thinking about that – I've got a sort of plan what to do. After all it isn't as if it was Dad's dolphin – it doesn't seem fair he should stop you from looking at it just because he used to be a Mooncusser and says the place is poisoned –

FEVER: Poisoned?

SYMPATHY: So I thought I could let you in very quietly while Dad's upstairs polishing the lamp –

GRITTY: Fine.

SYMPATHY: Then I'll go up and start arguing with him so as to keep him out of the way while you go down in the lift – Dad loves arguing, he'll do that for hours.

GRITTY: Won't you come down too, and see the dolphin?

FEVER [*simultaneously with* GRITTY]: We'd like you to come with us.

GRITTY: Besides, you'll need to show us how to work the lift.

SYMPATHY: Oh, that's easy; it's electronically controlled, you sing a tune to make the doors open, it was my dad's invention.

FEVER: Sing a tune?

SYMPATHY: Yes, he changes it every month. Just now it goes like this.

[*She hums lift music.*]

GRITTY: In that case you'll definitely have to come with us. My mate's tone-deaf and I can never carry a tune in my head – suppose we forgot it when we was down there –

SYMPATHY [*rather thrown*]: Oh. Well, we'll have to think of some plan to keep Dad out of the way, then.

GRITTY: That shouldn't be too difficult.

[*He ushers* SYMPATHY *out under umbrella while behind them* FEVER *pulls out a condensed-air gun and cocks it.*]

SCENE 9

The lighthouse. Remains of meal on table: teapot, loaf. SAUL *has constructed a trap to catch anyone coming through the door. It is a cage made of string and wicker, has a sliding trapdoor that drops down at one side. He is putting finishing touches to it, trying to get the slide to stay up. It keeps falling down. At present the cage – which is on castors – is in the middle of the room. Knock at outer door. Trapdoor falls again.*

SAUL [*crossly, over his shoulder*]: Wait, I'm not ready yet –

[*But the door opens.* LORD BOSS *and* SUNUP *come in.*]

SAUL [*angrily*]: Who are you? Get out. I never said you could come in. Get out, I tell you!

BOSS: We're from the Ministry.

SAUL: What Ministry?

BOSS: Ministry of Frontiers, Boundaries and Mysteries.

SAUL: I'll have no snoopers here.

BOSS: We have a trained Macaw, licensed to locate marsh gas, fire damp, poltergeists, atmospheric pollution and psychic phenomena.

SAUL: Get out.

BOSS: We've heard you're infested with ghosts here; we have an order to inspect.

SAUL: I order you to clear out.

[SUNUP *hauls on cord;* MACAWMACK *waddles in, looking very dejected.*]

SUNUP: Ah, have a heart; our hotel just fell into the sea.

SAUL: You can go and jump after it for all I care.

BOSS: And it's raining cats and dogs.

SAUL: One step farther and I shoot.

[*Snatches up blunderbuss, pulls trigger but misses, dislodges large mass of cobwebs which falls on him and the gun.*]

SUNUP [*gazing at the cage*]: What the dickens is that?

SAUL [*struggling out from under cobwebs; the gun is still hopelessly entangled*]: It's a daughter-catcher.

SUNUP: How does it work?

SAUL: Simple. My daughter's outside somewhere at the moment. I wheel it up to the door.

SUNUP: And she walks in?

SAUL: Straight into the trap; the slide falls, then I just wheel it outside with her in it.

SUNUP: I don't see how the sliding bit works.

SAUL: Like this. [*But when he turns to demonstrate,* SUNUP *shoots him with condensed-air gun, which makes a noise like water running out of basin. He falls, stunned.*]

BOSS: I *said* it would be easy. Why do I always end up on the job myself? Is he dead?

SUNUP [*examining*]: No. D'you want him dead?

BOSS: Not yet. We might need him to show us how to get down to the cave.

[*They dump him on armchair, cover him with drape of cobweb.*]

SUNUP [*looking round*]: That must be the lift. But there doesn't seem to be a call-button.

BOSS: Maybe it's on the next floor. Go up and see.

[SUNUP *goes upstairs to gallery, and then through door.* MACAWMACK *thoughtfully inspects cage and clambers in. The trap falls and shuts him in.*]

MACAWMACK [*dolefully*]: No exit. No way through. No way out!

BOSS: It's your own fault, you stupid bird. *I'm* not going to let you out.

[*He pokes* MACAWMACK *with a bit of cane;* MACAWMACK *pecks back like lightning and he only just leaps out of the way in time.*]

You can just wait till Sunup gets back. Hey! [*Calling upstairs.*] Have you found another entrance? Hurry up, the old guy will be coming to before long.

SUNUP [*reappearing on gallery*]: There's a woman asleep up here, me lord –

BOSS: Never mind her, have you found any doors?

SUNUP [*doubtfully*]: Nothing that looks like lift doors. I haven't been right up to the top of the tower – they say there's one thousand, two hundred and ninety-eight steps.

BOSS: I suppose I'll have to come – you wouldn't recognize the Atlantic ocean if you found it in your kitchen sink. [*He follows* SUNUP.]

MACAWMACK [*furiously battering at the cage*]: No parking, no lurking, no loitering, no smoking, no waiting, no skating, no talking, no boating, no joking, SILENCE, OPERATION IN PROGRESS!

SCENE 10

Same scene as previous: enter SYMPATHY [*in the lead*], GRITTY *and* FEVER.

SYMPATHY [*seeing* SAUL *lying in armchair*]: Sssh, Dad's asleep, that's a bit of luck.

GRITTY [*seeing* MACAWMACK *in cage*]: What's *that*?

SYMPATHY: Pet of Dad's, I suppose.

FEVER: Never mind him, where's the lift?

STMPATHY: Those doors.

FEVER: Let's have the tune then, miss –

GRITTY: Yeah, let's get down there while the coast's clear.

SYMPATHY: Um – [*She stands looking blankly ahead of her*] Pom, pom, pom, pom – no, that's not it; la, la, la, no; tiddle tiddle tum – I almost had it then; oh, this is so *stupid*; ten minutes ago I had it in my head clear as 'God Save the Queen'.

FEVER: You've gone and forgotten it?

SYMPATHY: It'll come back – I'm sure it will. It's a tune I know quite well.

FEVER: Yeah, and in the meantime old Whiskers there will wake up.

GRITTY: What about your mum, wouldn't she know the tune?

SYMPATHY: That's a good idea. She must be upstairs having her nap – I'll take her a cup of tea. [*She pours a cup from pot on table and goes upstairs and through gallery door.*]

MACAWMACK: Self-service only. Mind the step. Use this door. *Don't* use this door. All tickets to be shown. Look out for the platform. Put coin in slot.

GRITTY: Oh, be quiet. No one asked you to speak.

FEVER: Maybe we could get the lift doors open.

[*He tries to prise them apart; a little green smoke comes out.*]

GRITTY [*nervously*]: Hey, watch it; you might electrocute yourself; anyway it's no use if the lift isn't on this floor.

MACAWMACK: Beds, bedding, bathroom and all soft furnishings.

GRITTY: I've an idea, I'll try and get in touch with Caliban, *he* ought to know the tune – [*He pulls out pocket radio transmitter, switches on.*] Hullo, hullo, hullo Caliban, are you there, Caliban, calling Caliban, Caliban, can you hear me Caliban, calling Caliban –

[*His back is turned, he doesn't see* RUTH *coming downstairs; starts violently when she comes silently into his field of vision.* SYMPATHY *follows, running down with empty cup, guides* RUTH *to her rocking-chair.*]

SYMPATHY: You okay, Mum? Can I get you anything?

RUTH: No, dearie, thank you. Where's your father?

SYMPATHY: He seems to be asleep.

RUTH: At this time of day? That's funny.

SYMPATHY: Let's not disturb him.

RUTH: Isn't there somebody else here?

SYMPATHY: Oh – er – yes, it's – er – two friends of mine, Mum.

RUTH: What are their names?

[SYMPATHY *looks inquiringly at them; they murmur their names and she repeats.*]

SYMPATHY: Gritty and Fever, Mum – this is my mother.

RUTH: How do you do?

FEVER *and* GRITTY [*together, a little embarrassed*]: Pleased to meet you, ma'am.

RUTH: I'm afraid your father won't be pleased when he wakes, dear. He doesn't like visitors at all.

SYMPATHY: They needn't stay long.

RUTH: Where did you meet your friends?

SYMPATHY: Outside – just now.

RUTH: Before that, I meant; were they at ballet school with you?

SYMPATHY: Er – yes.

RUTH: Just fancy; so you're both dancers; did you get your diplomas at the same time as Sympathy?

GRITTY: That's right. [*He strikes a ballet posture, not being sure if* RUTH *can see anything or not.*]

FEVER [*who has been growing very impatient*]: Ma'am – we were wondering if you could help us with the tune that gets this lift working – your daughter said she would but she's forgotten it –

SCENE II

The lamp-room. SUNUP *and* LORD BOSS *totter in, exhausted from climbing all those stairs.* FRED, *surprised but pleased to see them, is already there.*

FRED [*singing*]:

Come unto this rockbound coast,
Every ghost;
Any spook who turns up here
Gets a beer;
Welcome, welcome to our shore,
There's always room for just one more,
  Hark, hark,
  Peek-a-boo,
  The owls do bark,
  To-wit-to-woo,

Hark, hark, I hear
Dolphins singing far and near,
A.E.I.O.U.

[SUNUP *and* BOSS, *insensibly influenced, begin to stagger about like zombies, then slowly subside into meditation posture and sit staring ahead of them.* FRED *strolls out.*]

SCENE 12

The lighthouse. Same as Scene 10. FRED *strolls down stairs.*

FRED: Company, I see. Fancy meeting up with old Fever again.

RUTH [*surprised*]: Do you know them, Fred?

FRED: The old one, I do; he used to be on the Yucatan straw-hat run with me in the old days.

RUTH: That's queer; he's a class-mate of Sympathy's; you'd think he'd be rather too old for a ballet student.

FRED: Old Fever a ballet student? You might as well teach a stalagmite to play hopscotch.

GRITTY [*to* SYMPATHY; *low voice*]: Is your mum all right? She's talking to herself.

SYMPATHY: She's talking to Uncle Fred's ghost.

FEVER [*in despair*]: Gawdamighty – ghosts, monsters, parrots – nutty old guys with whiskers – this is the screwiest job I ever was on –

RUTH: Your friends want to go down in the lift, dear, is that it, to the cave?

SYMPATHY: Yes, they're studying dolphins.

RUTH: Dolphins?

SYMPATHY: They want to – to make up a ballet about dolphins.

RUTH: But there aren't any dolphins down in the cave – only Caliban.

SYMPATHY: Caliban? [*Puzzled*] Who's Caliban? [*To* GRITTY] You were calling Caliban, Caliban, just now when I came downstairs – is Caliban the dolphin's name?

RUTH: No, Caliban's not a dolphin, lovey; he's something your father keeps down there in the cave.

SYMPATHY: A *person*? You mean father's got someone shut in down there?

RUTH: No, not a person – I'm not sure what he is.

SYMPATHY: But why's he there?

RUTH: Your father says there's an old book down there, sealed up in a lead box. Caliban thinks it belongs to him –

SYMPATHY: You mean to say, Father's pinched a book he's no right to, and he's got the real owner shut up down there –

RUTH: I believe he did once say he'd give it back, but then he changed his mind – he said it would only lead to trouble –

SYMPATHY: Isn't that just *like* Father – he's got no *right* to keep it. [*She starts towards* SAUL, *as if to shake him awake, but then an idea strikes her and she turns to* GRITTY.] Hey – did *you* know all this?

GRITTY [*embarrassed*]: Well –

FEVER [*impatient*]: Go on – tell her it's the book we're after.

SYMPATHY: You've been fooling me, haven't you? [*Furious.*] And I *liked* you - I really thought you wanted to help Mum and me – you've just been telling me *lies* – you and your dolphins' dreams.

GRITTY [*injured*]: Well, I *would* have helped you – anyway you've no call to act so superior, you've been telling lies yourself. [*Suddenly realizes the implication of this.*] Oh, *no* . . . [*He stares at* SYMPATHY *aghast, and pulls the wrapped ball out of his pocket.*] Here, hold this again for a moment, will you . . .

[*Puzzled, she takes it.*]

Anyway – so we *do* want the book – it certainly doesn't belong to your dad.

FEVER: And you do want to get your mum to a doctor.

RUTH: Dearie, I didn't realize that was what you were

planning – I don't think it would be any use at all – A doctor can't help me now.

SYMPATHY [*screaming*]: Oh, it's hot – why didn't you warn me. [*She drops the ball, which bounces into* RUTH'*s lap.*]

FEVER [*sourly to* GRITTY]: Now look what you've done, you've properly loused things up.

CALIBAN'S VOICE [*coming through amplified on* GRITTY'*s transmitter*]: Help, help, help, this is Caliban! Help me, help me, let me out of here. It's dark, I'm lonely! Please, please send someone to help me. Send me someone who's never told a lie –

[*There is an awestruck silence.*]

RUTH [*thoughtfully, half to herself*]: I could go and let that poor creature out.

SYMPATHY: *No*, Mum! He might be dangerous. You're not to!

FRED: He's got a very nasty temper, Ruthie, after being shut up all this time – I'd leave the job to someone else.

GRITTY: *Would* you do it, ma'am?

SYMPATHY: *No!*

FEVER: Look, we're all arguing – let's get the flaming *lift* up, eh? Can you sing us the tune, mum?

RUTH: Oh dear. Saul keeps changing it. Let's think now, is it the one that goes to Dublin's Fairy City? [*She sings* 'Cockles and Mussels', *but it isn't.*] It has something to do with the sea this month, I know –

SYMPATHY: 'Blow the Wind Southerly?' [*She tries.*]

GRITTY: 'What Shall We Do with the Drunken Sailor?' [*He has a go.*]

FEVER: 'Oh, I Do Like to be Beside the Seaside?' [*He joins in.*]

MACAWMACK: Lower the boats! Fire, fire! Avast the main brace! Women and children first! Crew members only!

[*At last he succeeds in raising the sliding door of the cage and clambers out, very excited;* FEVER *and* GRITTY *back away from him, still singing, but* SYMPATHY *tosses him the loaf from the table, which he takes briskly.*]

GRITTY *and* FEVER [*together, changing their tune*]:

The master, the swabber, the bosun and I,
The gunner and his mate
Loved Moll, Meg, Marian and Margery
But none of us cared for Kate.

[SAUL *rouses up at all this noise, staggers a few steps towards the cage and falls forward into it; the shutter falls again.*]

BOSS [*entering above on gallery, pointing gun*]: Keep quite still, the lot of you. Put your hands above your heads.

[*He yawns, still shaking off* FRED'*s influence; so does* SUNUP, *who has followed him in. Everyone puts hands over heads.* SUNUP *and* BOSS *come down. They have large plastic manacles like the rosette-type wall fitments that towels and teacloths are hung from; they simply jam one of these over each pair of hands. At this moment* SYMPATHY *by chance hits on the right tune and the lift music begins playing, light glows green. As the last pair of hands is secured, doors come open with cloud of green smoke.*]

BOSS: Sunup, get that bird into the lift. We'll take the girl, too – come on you [*to* SYMPATHY; *he pushes her into the lift and turns to say*] You'd better all keep quiet up here or I don't guarantee to bring the girl back with us.

[*Lift doors close.*
CURTAIN.]

ACT TWO

SCENE I

The cave. Long green filaments hanging from ceiling. Rocks here and there on the ground and a rock shelf at rear. Large bottle partially visible at one side, neck and huge cork protruding, with part of ship visible inside. Lift doors at rear as in lighthouse.

Doors open. LORD BOSS, SYMPATHY, *still with hands fastened,* SUNUP *and* MACAWMACK *emerge. Lift music. Doors close.*

SUNUP: Creepus, what a spooky hole. I don't like it down here, Boss, I'm scared.

BOSS: Oh, don't be so wet. What's going to hurt you?

[*A large crab clambers over his foot; he jumps back.*]

MACAWMACK [*sepulchrally*]: Private fishing. Bathing strictly forbidden. No landing. Dangerous undertow.

SUNUP [*irritably*]: Oh, do be quiet. You're no help at all. [*Looking round.*] Where d'you suppose Caliban is, then? He *asked* us to come down here – why don't he come out and say hullo?

BOSS: I daresay he's not far off. [*Calling*] Caliban! Caliban! Where are you?

[*They all call.*]

SUNUP, SYMPATHY *and* BOSS [*together*]: Caliban, Caliban, Caliban!

ECHO: Caliban, ibaniban, iban, iban, ban ban, ban . . .

SUNUP [*uneasily*]: Maybe that voice we heard over the transmitter was just an echo all along.

BOSS: Rubbish. Don't be stupid. You heard it answer, didn't you? It said things, it didn't just echo. Caliban, where are you? Why don't you come out? We've brought you someone who's never told a lie.

ECHO: Aye, aye, aye, aye, aye . . .

SYMPATHY: Oh, it's horrible here, it gives me the shivers. How *could* Father keep someone shut up down here? Caliban, *do* come out, we're all waiting for you.

MACAWMACK: Bring out your dead, bring out your dead!

SUNUP: Quiet, you stupid bird. Boss, I've had a thought. Maybe Caliban's shut up somewhere. Maybe he's inside the bottle.

BOSS: First sensible thought you've had since I've known you. Maybe he is.

SYMPATHY [*shivering*]: How're we going to get him out, then?

SUNUP: Break the bottle, I suppose. [*He bangs the bottle with his gun; no result.*]

BOSS: Why not pull out the cork?

[LORD BOSS *and* SUNUP *try to pull out cork, without success.*]

SUNUP: We might try bashing the cork with a big stone. [*He starts wandering about, looking for a suitable stone.*]

SYMPATHY [*studying the cork*]: There's words written on the cork.

SUNUP: I know. [*After a pause.*] What do they say?

SYMPATHY: Can't you read?

SUNUP: No. Can't you?

SYMPATHY: Well, yes – I can read English – but this is some foreign language – even the letters are peculiar.

[LORD BOSS *produces torch and shines it.*]

SYMPATHY: Can you move the light this way? Thanks – Uligarra – something – I'm not sure if that's right – yes, Uligarra-Zalgarra, that's it: Uligarra-Zalgarra. I wonder what it means? Oh –

[*With a tremendous amplified noise of glass breaking the bottle disintegrates and cork shoots out; explosion light-effect. In the middle of all this* CALIBAN *emerges. He is like a green gorilla, furry, with gills and web feet; his expression is both sad and malevolent.*]

SUNUP: Blimey, what a smell of fish.

BOSS: Are – are you Caliban?

CALIBAN: Are you dirty water, are you coal dust? Are you mud, are you offal, are you sweepings?

BOSS: Certainly not. My name is no affair of yours.

CALIBAN: And *my* name is my own affair. Caliban is what they call me, but Caliban is not my real name.

SUNUP: Well, there's no call to put on airs with us; what is your real name then?

CALIBAN [*cunningly*]: Aha. That I shan't tell you or it would give you power over me.

BOSS: Oh, very well, have it your own way.

CALIBAN: I *intend* to have it my own way.

BOSS: There's no need to take that tone with us; we've come to help you.

CALIBAN: How do I know that? No one has ever helped me. How do I know you're telling the truth?

BOSS: What would be the point of lying to you? We've come all this way on purpose to do you a good turn –

CALIBAN: The other one lied to me. He promised to use the book and then let me go. If he had used the book it would have set me free. But he lied. He never used it and he never freed me. He broke his promise.

SYMPATHY: That was my dad, I suppose. Sounds like him.

CALIBAN [*shouting, wagging his head from side to side, beating on his chest*]: Flout 'em and scout 'em and scout 'em and flout 'em. Ahhhhh! I hate you all, hate you, hate you, hate you!

[*He jumps towards them furiously and they scatter in fright.*]

SYMPATHY: But *we* haven't done anything bad to you, Caliban, why do you hate us? We've come here to help you.

CALIBAN: I don't believe you. You're all liars.

BOSS: That's not so. We'll *show* you that we're not liars. Only tell us where the book's kept –

SUNUP [*low voice to* LORD BOSS]: Suppose he don't know?

CALIBAN: Why should I tell you? Why should I give my secrets away?

BOSS [*impatiently*]: Oh, good heavens, what an oaf. Look here – we brought you someone who's never told a lie.

CALIBAN: I don't believe you.

BOSS: It's the absolute, stone-cold, glass-green, home-ground truth. That bird there has never told a lie in his life.

CALIBAN: I hate you, hate you, hate you.

SYMPATHY: Why do you hate us, Caliban?

CALIBAN: Because there's a whole world full of you – and there's only one of me.

BOSS: That's not our fault.

CALIBAN: Once the world was full of Calibans – now I'm all alone and I'm lonely, lonely, lonely – and you're all packed tight like rats.

BOSS: Just hand over the book and I'll make twenty more Calibans just like you – a hundred – *five* hundred, if you like – then you'll never be lonely again.

SUNUP [*low voice*]: Strewth, what a prospect . . . Hey, Boss, you don't really mean to do that?

BOSS [*low voice*]: Of course not, don't be more of a fool than you can help.

SUNUP: Why don't he use the book himself.

BOSS: Maybe he's like you – can't read. He doesn't seem very bright.

SYMPATHY [*to* CALIBAN]: Honestly, the bird doesn't tell lies. You could talk to him.

CALIBAN [*surlily addressing* MACAWMACK]: Where can I find another like me? Where can I find Caliban's mate?

MACAWMACK [*after considerable thought*]: Press Button B and get your money back.

CALIBAN: Treachery! Betrayal! I can see into your black hearts. You just mean to mock me. You thought you could steal Caliban's book and leave him alone in the dark. Didn't you? Didn't you? But you won't be able to use it and I'll never give it you, never, never, never.

SYMPATHY: Oh gosh, that really riled him. I'm scared. [*She turns and notices* FRED, *who has come in behind her.*] Uncle Fred! How did you get here? I never heard the lift.

FRED: I don't need to use the lift like you lot, I can come down whenever I fancy. Only I don't often fancy. But your mum asked me to drop down and see was you all right, she was getting nervous about you.

SYMPATHY: *I'm* getting nervous about me. What'll Caliban do, Uncle Fred?

FRED: I don't rightly know. I always did think your Dad was silly to keep him shut up. Now he's got out of his bottle, who's to say? Best climb up here, out of harm's way.

SYMPATHY: Could you get this thing off my hands, Uncle Fred?

FRED: Sorry, love, I can't manage that.

SYMPATHY: Well, could you sing the lift music? I can't, my t–t–teeth are ch–ch–chattering s–s–so.

FRED: I never was any good at getting electrical things to work. [*He tries but nothing happens.*] I darcsay Caliban's jammed it.

[SYMPATHY *scrambles up on rock ledge beside him; meanwhile* CALIBAN *is making darting attacks on* LORD BOSS *and* SUNUP, *which they dodge.*]

SYMPATHY: How is it I can see you, Uncle Fred, when I couldn't before?

FRED: I daresay you're in a state of shock.

CALIBAN [*to* LORD BOSS *and* SUNUP]: You think you're so wonderful because you can *think*. Where has thinking got you? Do you think you can get the better of me?

MACAWMACK [*who has retreated to the shelf with* FRED *and* SYMPATHY]: Danger! Keep away from live rail. Thirty thousand volts. Poison. High expolsive. High tension. Don't touch.

SUNUP [*dodging attack by* CALIBAN]: Boss! For heaven's sake! Why don't you shoot him?

BOSS: And lose my chance of finding the book?

[*Loud crash; coloured lights shoot upwards; dark.*]

SCENE 2

The lighthouse. GRITTY *is standing beside* FEVER, *jumping up and down so as to dislodge* FEVER'*s manacles with his head. He finally succeeds.* FEVER *takes* GRITTY'*s manacles off.* GRITTY *takes* RUTH'*s off.*

RUTH: Thank you.

GRITTY: Would you like a cup of tea, ma'am?

RUTH [*faintly*]: That would be nice. You'll find tea in the blue tin.

GRITTY: Make some tea, Fever, there's a good guy. [GRITTY, *meanwhile, goes to lift doors and sings lift tune over and over; nothing happens.*]

Why won't the blasted lift come up?

FEVER [*making tea*]: Maybe it's jammed. Maybe Caliban's done something to it down at the bottom. Maybe Boss left the doors open. Anyway – d'you *want* to go down?

GRITTY [*low voice*]: I feel bad about the girl.

FEVER: Dunno why. *You* were going to take her down, yourself, in the first place.

GRITTY: I know. But just the same I feel bad.

RUTH: Where's my husband?

[SAUL, *inside the cage, has just come to, staggered upright, shaken off drapery of cobwebs, and started furiously rattling the bars.*]

SAUL: Let me out, let me out, let me out.

FEVER: Oh, all right.

[FEVER *undoes the sliding door,* SAUL *bounds out of the cage and rushes to a large lever on the wall, which he pulls; there is a muffled distant explosion;* SAUL *then goes upstairs without taking any further notice of anybody.*]

GRITTY [*despairingly*]: Now you *have* done it.

FEVER: Done what?

GRITTY: Don't you see, you dumb fool, that was the lever that releases the rock that smashes the ship.

FEVER: Oh ... [*Slowly taking it in.*] You mean he's smashed up Boss and all below there.

GRITTY: Almost certainly.

FEVER: Ask me, that's not a bad thing; Boss and Sunup's no loss.

GRITTY: What about the girl? [FEVER *has made tea, hands him a cup; absently he passes it to* RUTH.] Here's your tea, ma'am.

RUTH: Thank you.

GRITTY: You've no call to thank us, ma'am; all we've done is bring trouble – your daughter's down in the cave with that monster – and Boss and Sunup, who aren't much better – let alone the fact that your husband has just pulled down a rock on them.

RUTH: Oh, it may not be too bad; I asked my brother-in-law's ghost to go down and keep an eye on her.

GRITTY: I don't see what a *ghost* can do. Ma'am, is there any other way of getting down to the cave, apart from the lift, which seems to be stuck?

RUTH [*dubiously*]: You could climb down the cliff I suppose. Then it rather depends how close the whirlpool is – it moves up and down the channel. Sometimes you can get past it, sometimes not.

GRITTY: Oh well, I might have a go. Here . . . [*He picks up long coil of rope, shakes off cobwebs, fastens one end round his middle and passes an end to* FEVER.] Just tie that round the stair-rail, will you? And do a clovehitch, none of your grannies. I'm going to have a bash at going down the cliff. See you at suppertime, I hope. [*He climbs out of the window.*]

[FEVER *thoughtfully considers the rope he is holding. He ties it to the stair-rail. Waits for a few minutes, then, equally thoughtfully, takes the bread-knife from the table and saws through the rope. Loud amplified twang! Distant splash.*]

SCENE 3

The cave. SYMPATHY, FRED *and* MACAWMACK *still on the ledge.*

SYMPATHY: My goodness, Uncle Fred, I *am* pleased you came down to keep us company. What do you think happened to the others?

FRED: I think that rock fell on them. [*He points to large rock occupying the spot where ship-in-bottle was before.*] In fact, I can see their feet sticking out.

SYMPATHY: Oh dear, Caliban too?

FRED: I can't see his feet. I rather think when the rock fell on those two, he got shot upwards; but I don't know where he is.

SYMPATHY: Poor Caliban.

FRED: Don't waste your sympathy on him; he's got a thoroughly disagreeable nature.

SYMPATHY: He's had a rotten deal, though. Suppose you'd been shut up all that time?

FRED: I wouldn't have minded; I'd have been a bit more pleasant about it.

SYMPATHY: Oh, Fred, how are we going to get out of here?

FRED: I dunno.

SYMPATHY: Macawmack, can't you say something useful?

MACAWMACK: Hold on tight. Have all fares ready, please. No dogs allowed. No children under fourteen. No musical instruments to be played in the subway.

SYMPATHY: That's no help. I only wish we did have a musical instrument. At least we could cheer ourselves up. We'll have to do exercises to pass the time and keep warm.

[*She stands, starts doing exercises which turn to arabesques, then she is dancing as well as she can with tied hands.* FRED *joins in doing a hornpipe.* MACAWMACK *flaps his wings. When* FRED *tires of dancing he sings.*]

FRED [*singing*]:

When nights are black with mist and murk,
That's when the Mooncussers get to work,
With pike and pick and spike and dirk
Behind each rock a bloke doth lurk,
And keels are split and hulls are stove
And wrecks cast up in every cove.
Why then we sing
Hey ding-a-ding
For this is the weather we approve.

SYMPATHY [*sinking exhausted on rock*]: This is a nice square rock. Hey – it has a lid – it's not a rock, it's a box –

FRED: Does it open?

SYMPATHY [*struggles to open lid*]: Yes, it's coming.
FRED: Anything inside? Pieces of eight?
SYMPATHY: No, it's a book – it must be *Caliban*'s book. Caliban – Caliban! Are you there? I found your book –
ECHO: Ook, ook, ook, ook . . .
FRED: That's useful. If you can read even the first word, I reckon it'll get us out of here.
SYMPATHY: Well I can't. I can't open it. It's padlocked.
[*Lights start to swing round and round.*]

SCENE 4

The lighthouse. RUTH *in rocking-chair.* FEVER *looking out of window.* FEVER *turns and approaches* RUTH.

FEVER [*in official voice*]: Madam, I am an official from the Ministry of Frontiers, Boundaries and Mysteries. I must inform you that we have been given to understand that your husband may be concealing stolen goods on these premises – namely a book of – um – historical value – and I have a warrant to search for it.
RUTH: Oh my goodness. Well – go on, search if you must – *I* can't stop you. But Saul won't be pleased. And, honestly, he gave up all that business *years* ago – I'm certain you won't find anything. Anyway, why don't you ask him? [*Calling*] Saul! Saul!
[*Sky outside window has become very dark. Thunder and lightning.* CALIBAN *appears outside window in flash of lightning; climbs in under cover of following dark and is then seen inside.* FEVER *sees him, is riveted with terror, then gives wild scream. He rushes for the window and jumps out. Loud amplified splash a moment or two later.*]
RUTH [*puzzled*]: What's the matter?
[CALIBAN *doesn't answer but stands with arms folded looking up the stairs.*]
RUTH: Saul! Saul! Could you stop polishing and come down

a moment? There's a man from the ministry here and I think he must have hurt himself.

[SAUL *comes out of door on to gallery.*]

SAUL [*irritable*]: Not *another*? I told the last lot to clear out.

[*He sees* CALIBAN, *is transfixed with terror but compelled to come on down. He slowly and reluctantly descends stairs, approaches* CALIBAN, *struggling against the compulsion, and crouches on the ground in front of* CALIBAN *with arms over head.* CALIBAN, *who has gathered up a thick mat of black cobweb, drops it over, completely covering him.* SAUL *gradually shrinks under it until it lies flat on the floor.*]

RUTH: Really I don't understand anything that's happening today. Saul? Are you there?

CALIBAN [*in* SAUL'*s voice*]: Yes, I'm here.

RUTH: Where's the man from the ministry?

CALIBAN: He's gone.

RUTH: Did he find the book he's looking for?

CALIBAN: It isn't here.

RUTH [*relieved*]: I told him it wasn't; I said you'd given up all that business long ago. What's happened to all the other people who were here before? Sympathy's school friends and the bird and those other people?

CALIBAN: Two of them are coming now.

[SUNUP *and* BOSS *come through the door, dressed in white versions of their previous costumes, with white faces like* FRED. *They seem dazed and confused.*]

SUNUP: Strewth, what happened? Where are we?

BOSS: I think we're in Rome airport. I want a first-class return to Pernambuco and a champagne cocktail.

SUNUP: *I* don't think we're in Rome airport. I can't see any news-stands. And I can't see my feet. I'm scared.

RUTH: Oh, you poor things. Don't you know what's happened to you?

[*They stare at her blankly.*]

RUTH: Well, at least you'll be company for Fred. Saul, could you pass me my knitting. I think it's on the table.

[CALIBAN *does so.*]

SCENE 5

The cave. Tremendous whirl of lights to represent whirlpool; they gradually slow down and come to a stop. GRITTY *drops down, reeling round and round, finally sinks to the ground.*

SYMPATHY [*who has been perched on rock, jumps off and runs to him joyfully*]: Gritty! How ever did you get down here?

GRITTY: Well, I started climbing down the cliff – but when I was nearly at the bottom the rope broke.

SYMPATHY: Heavens! You never fell through the whirlpool?

GRITTY: I reckon I must have. [*His hair's all in ringlets and the stripes on his shirt now go round him in spirals.*] Thought I ought to come down and see what was happening in here.

SYMPATHY: You came to rescue us! Oh, you are kind. Could you undo my hands? [*He does so.*] We're stuck, the lift won't work. And I found this book, but I can't get it open.

GRITTY: Caliban's book?

SYMPATHY: I suppose so. If we could find *him*, and give him the book, maybe he'd unstick the lift for us.

FRED [*despondently*]: If he's got out, I don't suppose anything will fetch him back again.

SYMPATHY: Surely he'd want to come back for his book? [*Calling*] Caliban? Caliban? Oh, I'm fed up with those echoes. [*She begins to dance a dance of evocation, stretching up her arms to call* CALIBAN *down from wherever he has got to.*]

GRITTY: I'll have a try on this thing. [*He sets up his little transmitter.*] Hullo, hullo, hullo, Caliban, are you there, Caliban, calling Caliban, can you answer me, Caliban, we've found your book, we've found your book, Caliban, over.

FRED [*singing*]:

> O Caliban, where are you roaming?
> O can't you hear, the wires are humming?
> Where's our monster got to now?
> Trip no more your monstrous measure,

Come back home, we've found your treasure,
Thought we ought to let you know.

[*They all go on doing their thing for some time. At last the light glows green.*]

SYMPATHY: Look, look –

[*Lift music; doors open. Green smoke.* CALIBAN *comes out. He is also now recognizably* SAUL. *Doors shut.*]

SYMPATHY: Father! [*More doubtfully.*] Are you Father? Or are you Caliban?

CALIBAN: Where is the book? Give me the book.

[CALIBAN *starts questing about; he looks so baleful that they retreat from him nervously and he becomes more and more menacing.*]

GRITTY [*who has picked up book and is holding it behind him*]: Now look here, Caliban – we have every intention of giving you the book, but will you guarantee us safe conduct up to the lighthouse if we do?

CALIBAN: No bargaining! [*He dives at* GRITTY *and manages to grab the book.*] Aha! Now! *Now* I have you all at my mercy. Now I shall go back into the world and wreak vengeance. I shall mow down the forests like mustard and cress. I shall trample the cities like carpets. I shall drink up the oceans like – lemon squash. [*He swaggers about threatening.*]

FRED: Oh no you won't, chum. Don't be silly. You may have the book but you still haven't got the key.

SYMPATHY: Besides which, I don't believe you can read.

GRITTY: So just pipe down and behave in a reasonable manner, will you?

MACAWMACK: Stand on the right. Hold on to the rail. Dogs and pushchairs must be carried.

CALIBAN [*stares threateningly at them for another minute, then gives a long, lugubrious wail*]: Oh, it's true, it's true! I haven't got the key. It's lost . . .

[*He completely caves in, sits down on a rock, hugging the book to his chest, wailing, and rocking backwards and forwards. Lift music begins softly, then louder; the lift doors open;* SYMPATHY,

GRITTY, FRED *and* MACAWMACK *file into the lift; the doors close;* CALIBAN *continues to sit and wail. Lights gradually dim to darkness.* FRED *comes in again, spotlit; he pats* CALIBAN *awkwardly on the shoulder.*]

FRED: *Do* cheer up, old fellar.

[*But* CALIBAN *continues to wail;* FRED *waits a moment, shrugs, then goes out.*]

SCENE 6

The lighthouse. RUTH *knitting;* LORD BOSS *and* SUNUP *have skipping-ropes and are seriously skipping and counting.*

BOSS: Thirty-seven, thirty-eight, thirty-nine, blast ... [*He trips over his rope and starts again.*] One, two, three ...

SUNUP: Seventeen, eighteen. [*He skips much more slowly.*]

[FEVER *comes in, also white.*]

FEVER: What the blazes is going on? I feel all queer. Light-headed. Have we all got yellow-fever – you two look very peculiar.

RUTH: Gracious, is that another of them?

SUNUP [*cheerfully*]: Hullo, old Fever, come to join the party? What happened to you? Where's Gritty?

FEVER: I dunno. The last thing I remember is falling over the cliff. Am I delirious?

BOSS: Not delirious. Just dead.

RUTH: Fred *will* be pleased to have so many new friends. He never complained, but I know he felt it that Saul never took any notice of him.

[*Lift music. Light glows green. Doors open.* SYMPATHY, GRITTY *and* MACAWMACK *burst out. Doors shut.* FRED *ambles through the ordinary door.*]

SYMPATHY [*running to* RUTH, *hugging her*]: Are you all right, Mum?

RUTH: Of course I am, dearie, I've got all this company to keep me cheerful. Somebody kindly made me a cup of tea.

SYMPATHY [*looking round*]: Gosh!

FRED [*with satisfaction*]: We'll be able to play bridge on winter evenings.

BOSS [*peevish*]: That I should end up playing bridge in a lighthouse with the ghost of a straw-hat smuggler. What a come-down.

SYMPATHY: But poor old Dad. Will he always stay down there in the cave with his miserable old grouch and his miserable old book?

RUTH: Oh, I daresay he'll come up one day. And in the meantime I expect Fred will go down and keep him company sometimes, won't you Fred?

FRED: Sure.

GRITTY: Maybe somebody will find the key to the book some day.

FRED: Dunno whether *that* would be such a good thing.

MACAWMACK: Place bag in locker, place coin in slot, turn key in lock.

RUTH: Now, dearie, it's long past teatime, you'd better be on your way or you'll miss the last bus.

SYMPATHY: Me? But aren't you coming, Mum? To see a doctor about your eyes?

RUTH: No, dearie. It's too late for that. Being blind isn't so bad.

SYMPATHY: Then I'll stay here and look after you.

RUTH: That wouldn't do, lovey. You need to go back to town, where there's theatres for your dancing. I'll be all right. And you can always come home on a visit.

SYMPATHY [*distressed*]: But who'll look after you? And the lighthouse?

RUTH: The young man will.

GRITTY [*simultaneously with* RUTH]: I will. It's just the sort of life that suits me. Plenty of time to sit in the sun and make up songs.

SYMPATHY: But Mum –

GRITTY: I'll keep an eye on her, Sympathy, don't you worry. You go and have your career, be a famous dancer.

SYMPATHY: Don't *you* want a career?
GRITTY: Not on your life!
[*He starts singing; they all join in.*]

I have other fish to fry,
Where the cow slips, there slip I,
Up in the lighthouse tower so high,
Snug as a mouse in an apple-pie,
– Till the arrival of some other guy,
Oh, how contentedly will we exist,
Shining our light through the murk and the mist,
Shining our light through the murk and the mist.

[*All the ghosts,* GRITTY, *and* MACAWMACK *begin to dance.* SYMPATHY *looks at them rather wistfully, longing to join in, but* RUTH *kisses her goodbye so conclusively that she goes out, though stopping for many backward looks.*
CURTAIN.]

THE MOONCUSSER'S DAUGHTER

Songs

WORDS BY JOAN AIKEN
MUSIC BY JOHN SEBASTIAN BROWN

Who Is Caliban

This song is from pages 90 and 94

Eels he has where he oughta have hair,
Hands and feet are suckers,
Breathes in brine instead of air,
Makes a horrible ruckus,
Sounds like a boiler in bad repair.

Let's leave Caliban, let him lie,
It's tough enough to be him,
No use dragging him high and dry,
Nobody wants to see him,
Bye, bye, Caliban, bye bye bye.

FULL FATHOM FIVE

This song is from page 92

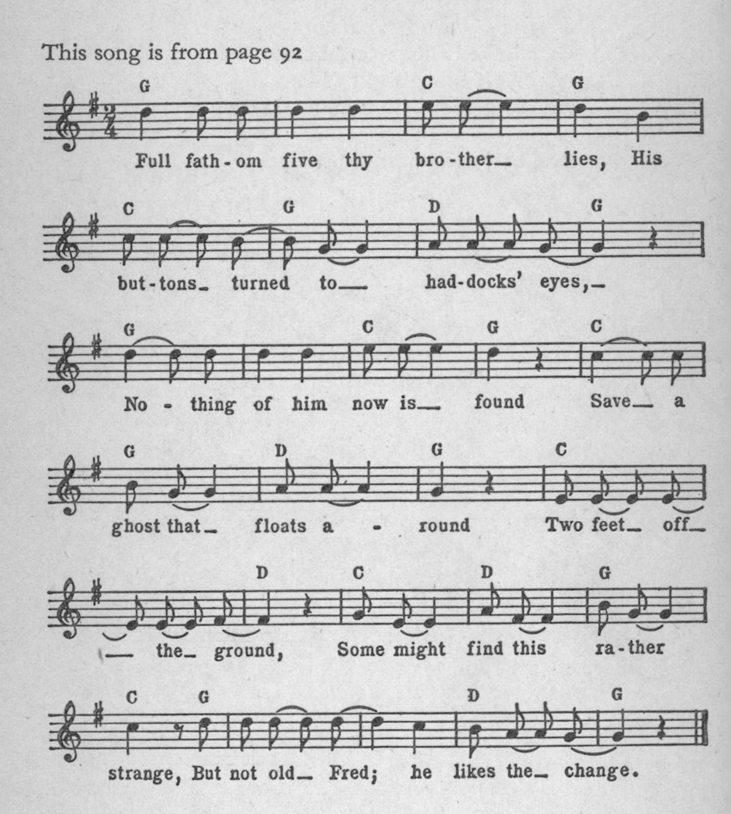

WHO DOTH NOT WANT A THING

This song is from page 95

MOONCUSSERS' SONG

This song is from pages 101 and 124

When nights are black with mist and murk,
That's when the Mooncussers get to work,
With pick and pike and spike and dirk
Behind each rock a bloke doth lurk,
And keels are split and hulls are stove
And wrecks cast up in every cove.
    Why then we sing
    Hey ding-a-ding
For this is the weather we approve.

Patience

This song is from page 105

C F G
Tell me— where is— Pa-tience mus - tered,

F G F G
How can— you stop from get-ting— flus - tered,

F. G
How re - main as— cool as— cus - tard?

C F G
You must learn to— med-i - tate,

F G F G
Don't be— so— pre - ci-pi - tate,—

F G
Ev-'ry-thing comes to— chaps as— wait,—

C G F
Play it by ear,— work to— rule,— What-

G C G C
-ev-er— hap - pens, keep your cool, Keep your cool.

Come Unto This Rockbound Coast

This song is from page 111

Repeat last three bars several times.

KATE

This song is from page 115

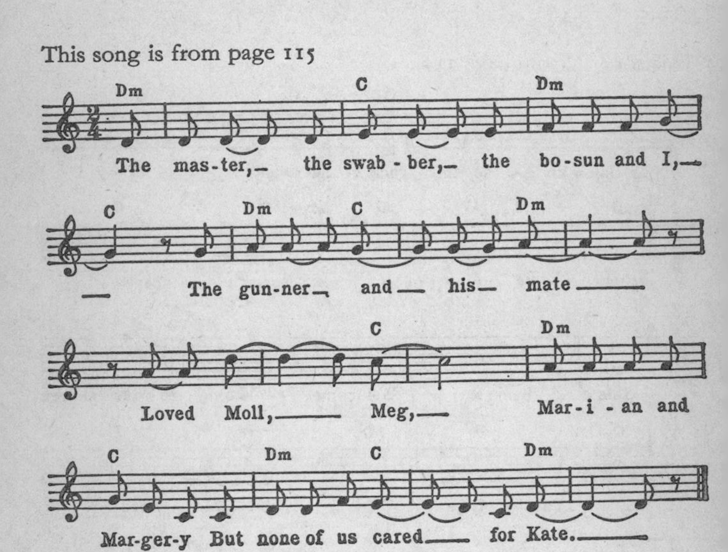

O Caliban

This song is from pages 127–128

Lighthouse Song